Also by John T. Kirk

Connecticut Furniture, Seventeenth and Eighteenth Centuries
1967

American Chairs, Queen Anne and Chippendale
1972

Early American Furniture

EARLY AMERICAN *Furniture*

HOW TO *Recognize, Evaluate, Buy,*
& Care For the Most Beautiful Pieces—
High-Style, Country, Primitive, & Rustic

by JOHN T. KIRK

ALFRED A. KNOPF

19 74

THIS IS A BORZOI BOOK
PUBLISHED BY ALFRED A. KNOPF, INC.

The epigraph is from "East Coker" in *Four
Quartets*, copyright 1943, by T. S. Eliot.
Reprinted by permission of Harcourt
Brace Jovanovich, Inc., and Faber & Faber Ltd.

Library of Congress Cataloging in Publication Data

Kirk, John T.
Early American furniture.

1. Furniture, American.   I.   Title.
NK2406.K56   1974   749.2'13   73–21822
ISBN 0–394–70646–3 (pbk.)

Manufactured in the United States of America

Hardcover Edition Published November 23, 1970
First Paperback Edition

This book is dedicated to
Elizabeth D. Kirk

That was a way of putting it—not very satisfactory:
A periphrastic study in a worn-out poetical fashion,
Leaving one still with the intolerable wrestle
With words and meanings. The poetry does not matter.

                    *   *   *

There is only the fight to recover what has been lost
And found and lost again and again: and now, under conditions
That seem unpropitious. But perhaps neither gain nor loss.
For us, there is only the trying. The rest is not our business.

                                        T. S. ELIOT

ACKNOWLEDGMENTS

On completing a book, it is the author's pleasure to thank those who have helped to make it relevant to the field, and to take upon himself the mistakes that may have been included inadvertently. No such book is a one-man creation. It is the product of all of those who have affected the author, and of all the material he has used, both the objects and the information about them.

First to be acknowledged are the actual pieces of furniture, their makers, and their original buyers. Then there are those who have preserved, collected, and published. Francis P. Garvan, as an insightful collector, has benefitted me the most, and therefore nearly half of the pieces included here are from his collection. Jules D. Prown, of Yale University, gave critical help in securing permission to publish many of the photographs, and the firm of Israel Sack, Inc., opened its files of photographs. I am particularly grateful to Donald A. Shelley, executive director, and to Katharine Hagler, both of the Henry Ford Museum and Greenfield Village, for their special attention to my problems and for making photographs so readily available. And to Pat Kane, of the Yale University Art Gallery; David B. Warren, of the Bayou Bend Collections; William V. Elder, III, of the Baltimore Museum of Art; Frank L. Horton, of the Museum of Early Southern Decorative Arts; Henry J. Harlow, of Old Sturbridge Village; J. Peter Spang, III, of Heritage Foundation, Deerfield; Alice Marvin, of the Shelburne Museum; and Berry B. Tracy and Mary C. Glaze, of the Metropolitan Museum of Art—all of whom made their objects easily accessible and contributed in various ways. I also wish to thank Danny Hingston and Richard W. Withington for making available photographs of primitive objects from the Oliver E. Williams sale. I regret that the manuscript was set in type before I could make reference to the recent, helpful contribution to the field, *Country Cabinetwork and Simple City Furniture*, edited by John D. Morse.

The private collectors who have played an important role are, particularly, Mr. and Mrs. Charles L. Bybee, who not only provided photographs but made their unusually exciting collections available for study in so many other ways. Mr. and Mrs. Bayard Ewing's collection of Rhode Island primitive material strengthened one of the sparser areas of study; in addition, "The Farm" provided the roof under which the final draft of this manuscript was written. Mrs. G. Dallas Coons and Frank Horton have been very helpful in discussing Southern furniture. And my appreciation of Norman Herreshoff's contribution is not confined to the use of his objects, but includes the benefits of a continuing discussion of what constitutes successful achievement in the medium of furniture.

Many dealers gave of their time and knowledge, but Roger Bacon has for ten years been my main informant and sounding board on primitive furniture, and Albert Sack has nearly embodied the high-style.

The American Philosophical Society provided a grant that made it possible to include hitherto unphotographed furniture, and I deeply appreciate their generosity. I must also include two mentors of different periods of study: Rigmor Andersen, of the Royal Danish Academy of Fine Arts, Copenhagen, who planted the idea that quality was the most important thing when studying furniture; and Meyric R. Rogers, Curator Emeritus of the Mabel

Brady Garvan and Related Collections, the Yale University Art Gallery, who furthered the idea. Of those outside the field, Daniel Robbins deserves special mention for revealing the relationship of modern painting and sculpture to early furniture. I am indebted to the First Annual Starksboro Conference both for its spark and what it started and for focusing on the special role of men in creating an aesthetic environment.

It is always impossible fully to thank those who helped in the physical construction of a book. Mrs. John W. Place has typed and retyped the manuscript endlessly and seen the whole project as a pleasurable adventure, helping me to do the same. Jane Garrett, who asked for the book, has quietly seen that so many potentially rough places have been eliminated, and Wendell Garrett has given helpful advice, some of which I have taken.

My final pleasure is to thank my wife, to whom this work is dedicated; she enjoyed, and endured, endless parades of furniture, helped to gather information from museum files, read and corrected the manuscript at various stages, and always gave the project insightful support. And then, of course, there is Natasha, who sat not only at my feet but on them.

J. T. K.

CONTENTS

Early American Furniture

INTRODUCTION

The ideas and areas of thought discussed in this book developed, in part, because I have found in lecturing on American furniture that audiences usually ask the same basic questions. There seems a need for a book that confronts directly many of the things that bother or puzzle people about American furniture, a good many of which are also what make it interesting. Too often books on the subject are generalized surveys, without detailed discussions of the "why," "when," and "how"—particularly "how." Then there are such questions as what to buy, how to buy, and how to take care of what is bought.

A second reason for my feeling that a book like this is needed can be summed up by an experience I had in a small antique shop near Shelburne, Vermont, a few years ago. On entering the shop, I saw a mediocre landscape painting from the mid-nineteenth century that interested me because of its beautiful green tones. The landscape as such had no great monetary or aesthetic value, but the color was just right for a room in the farm we then owned in New Hampshire. When I asked the price, however, I was told that it was very expensive because it was a "primitive." Obviously, this all but inclusive title had been chosen simply because the picture had been painted some time ago and lacked artistic merit. Indeed, it did lack aesthetic merit, but it also lacked any of the excitement, amusement, or rich pattern found in work correctly grouped as "primitive."

For many reasons Americans are ready to endow anything old with the accolade "antique," or "primitive," thereby raising it to financial and assumed aesthetic importance, the two being in-separable in some minds. By lumping things together in this way, the very factor that makes a great object great is often missed. With furniture, as with paintings, we overlook the fact that all good cabinetmakers had their off days, and that many minor craftsmen made furniture which should be recognized simply as old furniture. Truly great furniture, on the other hand, deserves to be on a par with great sculpture.

This, then, is a book which does not prize something simply because of its age; rather, it is interested in American furniture as art. Lying behind this emphasis on excellence is a feeling that American furniture must be divided into at least four types, or groups, which constitute four basic approaches to design: high-style, country, primitive, and rustic; and that each piece should be evaluated within its own group. This division is obviously not the only one possible; it is simply a way of getting at what is different about several types of design.

The text is not a chronological survey of furniture, but is arranged according to ideas, problems, and specialized groups. This means that the photographs under discussion are sometimes in different parts of the book, but since text and photographs are interdependent this has been minimized wherever possible. Also, because of the importance of comparisons, illustrations of related pieces in the same part of the book have been put on the same page, or on facing pages, so that they may be studied together, even when this means that the related text must be on a different page. Because of this, a guide indicating location of the text relating to each figure (plate) has been provided, preceding the Index.

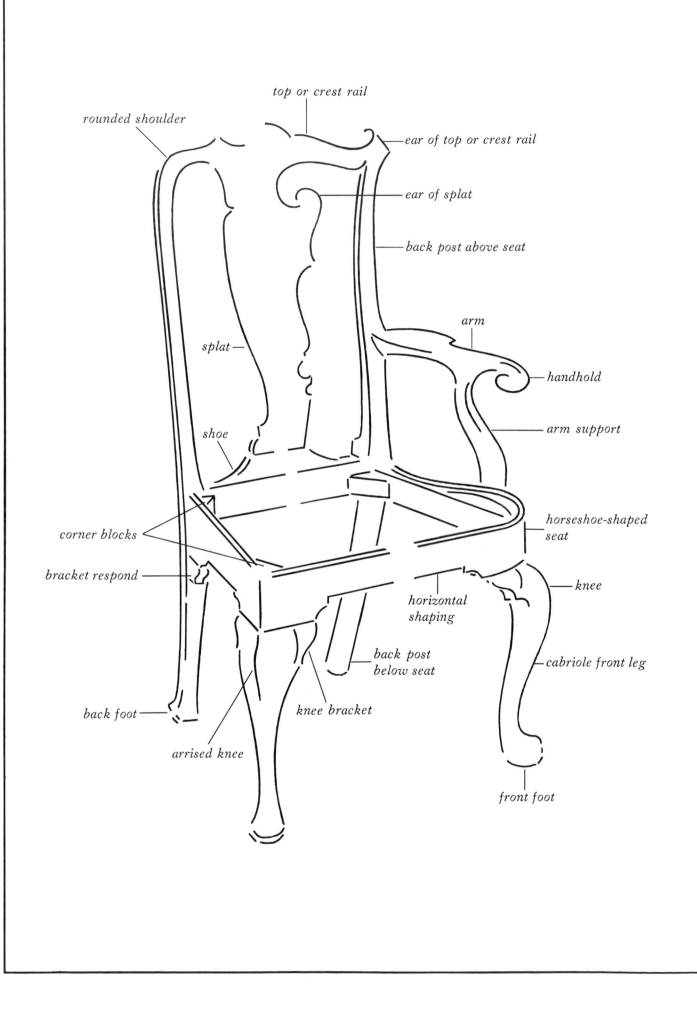

rounded shoulder

top or crest rail

ear of top or crest rail

ear of splat

back post above seat

arm

splat

handhold

arm support

shoe

corner blocks

horseshoe-shaped
seat

bracket respond

knee

horizontal
shaping

back post
below seat

cabriole front leg

back foot

knee bracket

arrised knee

front foot

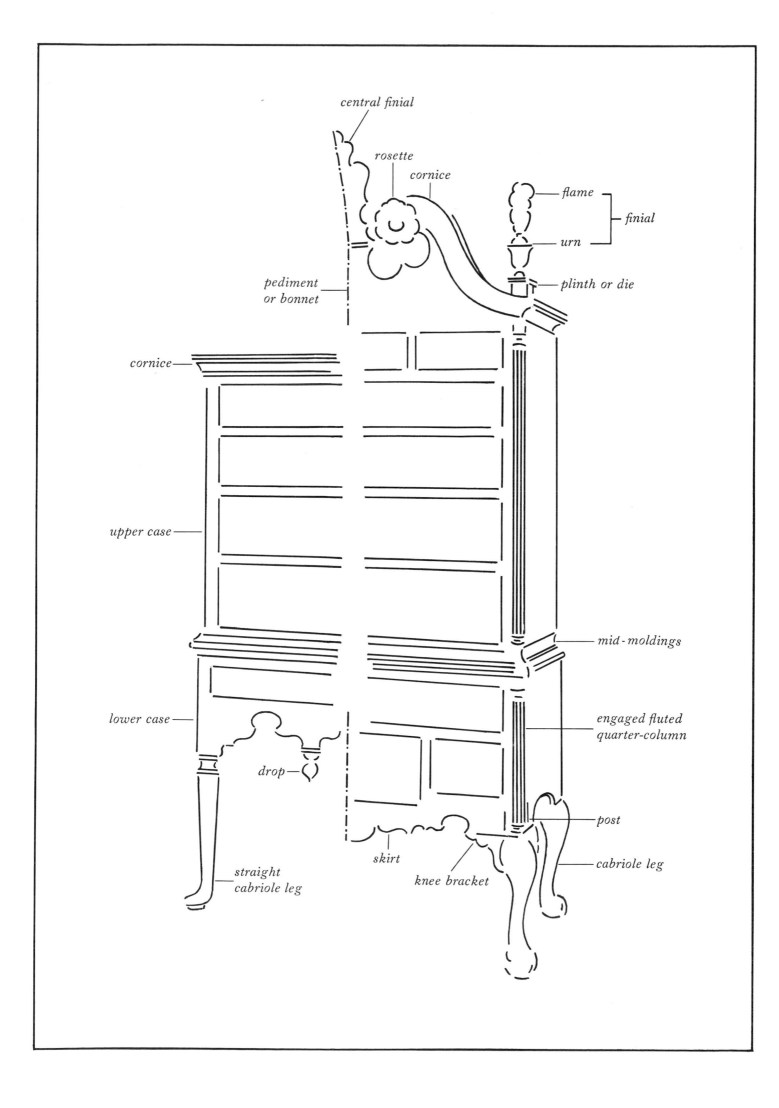

central finial

rosette

cornice

flame

finial

urn

pediment
or bonnet

plinth or die

cornice

upper case

mid-moldings

lower case

engaged fluted
quarter-column

drop

post

cabriole leg

straight
cabriole leg

skirt

knee bracket

Chronology of American Furniture Forms

Forms	General Date Blocks
Early Seventeenth-Century Furniture	1630 to 1680
Late Seventeenth-Century Furniture	1670 to 1710
William and Mary Furniture	1700 to 1735
Early Ladder-Back Chairs	1690 to 1720
Early Bannister-Back Chairs	1700 to 1735
Late Ladder-Back Chairs	1710 to 1800
Very Late Ladder-Back Chairs	1780 to 1880
Late Bannister-Back Chairs	1720 to 1800
Queen Anne Furniture	1730 to 1760
Early Queen Anne	1730 to 1750
Late Queen Anne	1740 to 1760
Country Queen Anne	1730 to 1800
Primitive Queen Anne	1730 to 1805
Composite Queen Anne and Chippendale Furniture	1745 to 1795
Chippendale Furniture	1755 to 1795
Straight-Leg Chippendale	1760 to 1795
Country Chippendale	1755 to 1810
Early Classical Revival Furniture	1790 to 1815
Late Classical Revival Furniture	1810 to 1840
Greco-Roman Revival Furniture	1810 to 1845
Early Greco-Roman Revival	1810 to 1820
Late Greco-Roman Revival	1815 to 1845
Fancy Furniture	1800 to 1840
French Restoration Style Furniture	1830 to 1850
Rococo Revival Furniture	1845 to 1870
Early Windsors	1755 to 1810
Bamboo-Turned Windsors	1805 to 1875

CHAPTER I

Taste, Design,
Construction,
&
Function

1. Side chair, Maryland, Annapolis or Baltimore, 1790–1815. *Yale University Art Gallery; The Mabel Brady Garvan Collection.*

In discussing furniture, it is always tempting to talk about the role of the materials and, even more, to emphasize the use to which various objects were put. Our industrial age tends in any case toward this particular rational approach, but in fact throughout the history of design the dominating taste of the moment has been *the* powerful, all-controlling factor in creation. It is taste that changes the design of women's clothes, just as it is taste that changes architectural design. True, without the technical achievement of plate glass, contemporary buildings could not exist; but the demands of taste generally bring into use the new materials at the moment when they are technically feasible. Similarly, if we are to understand an individual piece of furniture, we must approach it from the point of view of the prevailing taste.

American seventeenth- and eighteenth-century furniture played an extremely important role in its environment; it acted as its sculpture. Little true sculpture was made on these shores until well into the nineteenth century, but the three-dimensional furniture that filled the rooms more than sufficed in its place. Furniture stood out in relief if placed against a wall, and people walking around, looking through or beyond it, participated in endless ways in its being. Further, furniture was an active member of a household and revealed much about its owner. It was a vital backdrop to his life; it formed the main part of his artistic property, indicating his taste, wealth, and station. It was a symbol, as well as being useful. Thus, the well-to-do sought the latest mode, and the desire for prominence and elegance often ruled an owner able to afford change. Even when it was necessary to design the interior of a piece to fit a special need, the exterior was made to harmonize with prevailing "correct" design. There were, of course, those who decided for personal reasons to have things made which continued the style of an earlier period; and there were others who, because of aesthetic preference or religious scruples, had things made in a special way. But the majority chose the most fashionable surroundings they could afford. They wanted their homes to appear similar to, or better than, those of their friends.

Each period, each change to a new expression of style, has its own atmosphere, its own *ungrund*, a sense of fitness which is seen in everything that makes that period itself: in the arts, in thought, customs, clothing, and the myriad other things going on at any given moment, whether conscious or unconscious. All this combines to create a particular, recognizable milieu. And because each period has such totality, objects whose exact date of creation is unknown can be assigned a time by understanding their approach to design and associating it with a period of similar impact.

The second major factor in design is the materials used and the means of construction available, and the interplay or interaction between them.

Construction, which seems so basic an element of furniture design, is always at the mercy of aesthetic demands. For example, the case furniture first built on these shores in the early years of the seventeenth century used the age-old tradition of frame construction in oak. The chest—that primary unit of all furniture—had strong corner posts connected by heavy rails and central vertical stiles; the resulting open areas were filled with panels (see figure 28). The vertical and horizontal members were soundly united by mortise and tenon joints secured with pins, producing an object so firm and sturdy that it could have been rolled down hills without serious damage. This method of construction pervaded everything at the time. Even contemporary wood houses had big corner posts connected by sills and girders, which were in turn connected by thin uprights or studs, and the open areas filled with brick, or wattle and daub.

Typical of the large case pieces of the seventeenth century, the press cupboard from Connecticut made about 1690, figure 27, has strong corner posts united by horizontal rails enclosing panels, and the entire façade is elaborately decorated. This piece is constructed of such massive members that it would withstand great physical abuse. The form of construction was a basic factor in its design; it produced the necessary sturdiness, and its visibility was a strong factor in the piece's aesthetic impact. But, as taste changed, construction followed suit.

The William and Mary style that came immediately after this sturdy seventeenth-century style produced the most fragile of case-piece construction. The new style reflected the baroque taste that had traveled up the European continent to the Lowlands, thence to be transferred to England by the returning monarch, Charles II, and further elaborated after the eventual arrival of William and Mary. This style depended for its pattern upon movement from thick to thin, an alternation between massive, bulging areas and slender elegant parts, producing great curves that formed rich, ornate, plunging patterns. When the fashion reached the colonies from England in about 1700, the grand generous movement, like all styles transferred here before about 1800, had been simplified for its new provincial setting. Such simplified continental baroque curves are seen in the base of the highboy in figure 68. The slender baluster turning is capped with a spreading cup form, and the skirt moves in a counterpoint of curves across the base of the lower case; the shape of the flat stretchers picks up the movement of the skirt, repeating its curves on the horizontal plane. While the base is the most elegant area of the design, it utilizes what is perhaps the most ridiculous type of construction ever instituted in the history of furniture making. The baluster leg which joins the case is simply connected to it by a dowel-like pin between the leg and the skirt of the stand; similarly, the leg is connected through the stretcher into the foot by another dowel-like member. Today, comparable

pieces that have not been reworked and tightened can, if the upper case is pushed back and forth, move within a radius of some two to three inches. Stability, dominant for hundreds of years, was superseded by the taste for a new elegance that demanded slender, high-perched forms. An attitude, a pattern, an eye-pleasing arrangement was achieved while the very thing that makes furniture usable as furniture was sacrificed. The same visual effect could have been achieved with more stability had the leg been made one piece with the corner post of the lower case, a form of construction that immediately followed in the Queen Anne period (see figure 12).

In the Queen Anne style the heavy counterpoint movement of William and Mary gave way to what Hogarth in England called "the line of beauty"— the reverse curve that opened out, was attenuated and softened to form a long, gently flowing S-shape—and a more adequate form of construction was introduced. The cabriole legs are one piece of wood with the corner posts of the lower case; and, although this style is characterized by a more gentle, fluid, graceful movement which would seem to ask for a more gentle form of construction, the sound seventeenth-century principles of construction have been reintroduced. The reverse curve of the legs is carefully oriented so that the grain of the wood is lined up under the corners of the great weight they must support. The corner post is placed directly over the ankle, and the knee over the foot: the curve of the leg moves out at the knee and back again to be behind the knee as it arrives at the ankle; from there it thrusts forward again to place the foot directly under the knee. At times the front faces of the corner posts are veneered to look as if they are a separate piece (see figure 26), but this is only an artificial device to make the exterior, or visible part, conform to the taste for enrichment while sound interior construction is maintained. This decorating of the surface of an object in a way that does not reflect its structure developed throughout the ensuing styles.

The transition from sound construction through a ridiculous phase and back to another sound practice is found also in chairs of the late eighteenth century. Chippendale chairs of the second half of the eighteenth century were sturdily built, but in about 1800 new ideas resulted in flimsy construc-

2. Side chair, Maryland, Annapolis or Baltimore, 1790–1815. *Yale University Art Gallery; The Mabel Brady Garvan Collection.*

3

tion. Figure 1 shows an oval-back chair made in Maryland between 1790 and 1815. To construct an oval back, the cabinetmaker needed four pieces of wood: top and bottom members with grain that ran horizontally, and two side members with grain running vertically. Wood is strongest along its grain; when the long fibers are cut through to produce a curve, the resulting short grain snaps easily, separating along its short fibers. This oval-back chair has been repaired many times, and the repairs are always where the grain is shortest; that is, near the joints, or at the "corners" of the oval. Simply put, the oval form in thin wood is not a practical design unless the wood members are steamed and bent as in bow-back Windsor chairs (see figure 169), where the grain runs up and around the entire back. Such Windsors can utilize a circular movement because the nature of the material is taken into account, but oval forms constructed of many unbent pieces are impractical. That these designs were attempted shows once again the power of taste—a desire for the current fashion which overrode sound methods of construction. The side chair in figure 2 was also made in Maryland, and uses many of the same design elements. But its back is basically a shield-shaped square, which allows a sounder means of construction that does not violate the nature of the material. In England, oval-back chairs by the great designers such as Robert Adam were made of heavier parts or upholstered so that they could be constructed of broad pieces, which were then padded and covered with cloth.

Once taste has altered structure to meet its demands, there is often much interplay between the two as new ideas are worked out. Figure 3 shows a Philadelphia-type Queen Anne side chair with a squared seat frame. The lower edge of the seat frame rises between the knee brackets in double reverse curves, which make it lighter. This allows a large, long mortise and tenon joint between the seat rails and the upper part of the leg, and the

3. Side chair, Pennsylvania, probably Philadelphia, 1730–1750. *Yale University Art Gallery; The Mabel Brady Garvan Collection.*

shaping or cutting away of the seat rail along the lower edge responds to the taste for a thinner section across the middle of the skirt. Had the seat rail been left unshaped (the same dimension from one corner post to the other), it would appear awkwardly deep. Here taste and sound construction are working hand in hand. The developed Philadelphia Queen Anne style that followed (see figure 106) employed a multitude of reverse curves which made it desirable for the seat rail itself to curve. The splat is cut to multiple reverse curves; the back posts are shaped to reverse curves, when seen both from the front and the sides; and the seat is similarly shaped to move out from the back posts and over the front legs in a horseshoe configuration. The whole chair is a sculptural form utilizing the most graceful curves in a symphony of blended movement. Here taste has created a superb statement, and construction has successfully followed suit.

The new swing out over the front legs in chair design meant that a greater depth of wood was necessary to supply the projecting front corners. The cabinetmakers of Philadelphia, and a few in Connecticut, followed an English practice that utilized this new depth. They joined the side and front seat rails to each other in a deep, massive joint, and then pegged the front leg up into it. Because of this horizontally deep joint, the seat rail no longer needed vertical depth at its front corners, as in figure 3, since the seat rails no longer were tenoned into the corner posts. The rails, then, became vertically slender, and the horizontal shaping which had lightened the center disappeared. A style of seat that moved in rhythmic curves out over the front legs had made extra wood available for a new kind of joint; the new joint then made it possible to peg the leg in from below, and removed the need for vertically deep joints and thus horizontal shaping. Not all areas of America thought alike. Only the Philadelphia cabinetmakers and a few from Connecticut, perhaps influenced by Philadelphia, were sophisticated enough to reach this subtle level of chair design. Elsewhere the possibility of such a seat form was ignored and seat rails continued to be tenoned into the tops of front legs as in figure 107. When the desire for a squared seat frame returned to fashion, when straightness played a major role in the

Chippendale taste, the earlier practice of using horizontally shaped seat rails, with deep tenons fastening into the tops of the front legs, reappeared (figure 113).

The third major aspect of furniture design is function. Desks had to open; chairs had to be sat on; tables had to be unfolded for tea, cards, dinner, or writing. Furniture had to be useful, in addition to being fashionable sculpture. Like architecture, it was required to be both functional and beautiful, but of the two, the aesthetic was the more powerful. Just as taste dominated construction, it often demanded that the particular use the object was meant to serve should be disguised. In seventeenth-century furniture, it is usually possible to understand the interior spaces of a piece from the exterior pattern. In figure 28, for example, we clearly see a chest section over a drawer. But by the beginning of the eighteenth century, the ready understanding of interior spaces was often difficult. The piece in figure 69, reflecting the new taste, appears to have five ungraduated drawers when, in fact, it has the same basic interior spaces as figure 28, but disguised to look like a full chest of drawers. The upper section, with its façade made to look like two drawers, is actually a chest with a lift lid. Since past habits are not as easily broken as former taste, the owner still wanted a chest for storing clothes. But the object when viewed had to look fashionable. The solution suited the demands of both taste and practicality.

The tension between use and appearance continued to plague the designer-maker. Figure 43 shows a chest-on-chest made late in the eighteenth or early in the nineteenth century. The three "small drawers" placed side by side in the top tier and the three at the base or bottom tier are only pseudo small drawers; each, in fact, is one long drawer, masked with applied rectangles to appear smaller. Not only are these long drawers disguised to suit the notion of how a large piece should look, but the lower two long drawers are really one very deep drawer made to look like two from the outside. Again function has been maintained while the exterior echoes more dominating demands. Had this piece been made to reflect its interior spaces (that is, with a series of long drawers, one of which was extremely deep) it would have *looked* awkward.

CHAPTER II

The Evolution

of Style

Taste is continually changing, evolving, continually creating a fresh sense of rightness and appropriateness, and is itself constantly being modified by these elements. Generally speaking, a designer or purchaser accepts the authority of any expression that originates from a place he feels to be a source of culture. For Americans during the time we are considering, this was to a great degree England, which, in turn, accepted inspiration from various Continental sources. To the colonists, England was home; it was the mother country, and it was the accepted creator of taste. Virtually every form, every detail, and every method of construction used by the colonists had its source there. (This does not mean that English and American objects are indistinguishable, for they are no more alike than English pieces and their Continental sources.)

Throughout the history of furniture, in America as elsewhere, there has been a constant shifting, a continual movement between two fundamental attitudes toward form: one, the rectilinear, squared effect, and the other, the curvilinear. In the seventeenth century, furniture was composed of squared, sturdy, rectilinear forms; and the majority of pieces, when elaborated, were decorated with very shallow, flat "two-plane" carving—that is, there was a background, a recessed area, and a front area level with the wood panel around the decoration. There was little or no sense of roundness. The square, hard forms have a shallow or applied surface ornamentation and everything seems controlled within the squared edges of the piece (figure 28). In the William and Mary period that followed (1700–1735), much of this flat, rectilinear quality is maintained on large surfaces, but it begins to enclose movement. The upper section of a case piece is decorated with veneer which, although flat, is patterned, and acts rather like the low relief carving of the century before but with greater elegance; in the legs, too, a more baroque sense of movement is found (figure 68). The chairs of the period do allow for more all-over movement, but the backs are often flat.

In the Queen Anne period (1730–1760), the movement toward the curve is completed; the multiple curves and their counterpoint create the open, graceful shapes that are so prized today (figure 12). With the coming of the Chippendale period (1755–1795), square rectilinear forms were reintroduced, and in the chair acted as a foil to the pulsating details of the splat. This rococo period is the most frenzied of eighteenth-century styles. But in America the basic shape or unit of case furniture is seldom curved as it would be on the Continent. For example, an elaborate Philadelphia case piece such as that in figure 17 is, if stripped of its ornamentation, simply a box with drawers, on a stand with drawers, on stocky, reverse-curve legs.

During the next stage, the classical revival designs of 1790 to 1815, there is a return to the earlier defining of space in squares. Although this style uses shields, ovals, and tapered and round legs, it delineates rectilinear units almost brittlely (figure 16). In the Greco-Roman Revival which followed (1810–1845), there is another shift to the moving line (figure 41); and the next basic group of styles, usually lumped together as Victorian (1845–1870), reintroduces open movement. The great pulsating line that the Continent knew in the baroque and rococo throughout the eighteenth century is finally achieved. In America rich taste was only hinted at in the William and Mary, Queen Anne, and Chippendale styles; but by the mid-nineteenth century, forms were being dissolved in complete movement and the basic structure became one with the deco-

ration; the great curves of Victorian furniture form at once the decoration and the substance behind it; they serve as both elaboration and construction. During the late 1860's, squareness was reaffirmed until *art nouveau* redissolved it even more than before in a deliberate and delightfully awkward elegance. In the early twentieth century, the Bauhaus reintroduced the square. Not until the fifties, with the introduction of such furniture as Saarinen's single-leg plastic chairs, do we return to the great sweeping curve, a neo-*art nouveau*.

Shifts in style progress continually as tastes change, but during the seventeenth and eighteenth century America was far removed from its source of inspiration and the changes in furniture design came about slowly. In silver they were more rapid. Emigrants from Europe usually brought their silver with them; it was small, easily portable, and often represented a considerable portion of their wealth. The new styles imported were quickly utilized by American silversmiths. Furniture was not so easily transported, however, and although English designs continued to be imported by those who wanted truly to emulate the Europeans, furniture did not represent a source of wealth. It could easily be purchased here and by the sixth decade of the eighteenth century American products were considered preferable, unless you wanted craftsmen to brand you "Tory." After 1790, English pattern books made for more rapid style changes, but the earlier American craftsmen took nearly all their ideas from objects, not books. Although a new style could arrive suddenly and be found in a few thoroughly new products, the majority of makers moved gradually from one style to another.

This general gradualness of change is demonstrated by figures 4 through 8. The chest of drawers, figure 4, uses the form of decoration known as

4

"blocking" to enrich its front façade. It is organized in three strong vertical units: the two side units project in rounded curves, and the center section is a flat recess with curved ends; the bottom molding, like the top, follows the form of the front, and it rests upon reverse-curve bracket feet; the knee brackets curve to follow the curve above. The whole piece is carefully integrated—top, front, bottom molding, feet, and knee brackets each responding to the other areas. The front face, although strongly accented to three verticals, is counteraccented by the strong horizontals of the four drawers and the three boards that separate them, which are edged with a bead molding giving them greater emphasis. Each of the twelve rectangular areas created by the horizontals and verticals is centrally accented by large, shaped brass plates. Those of the central rectangles are placed near the top of the drawer. This accommodates the lock, which must be near the top of the drawer, and simultaneously creates an arching effect when each escutcheon is seen in relation to its flanking handles. But this does not occur on the top drawer, which thus relates to the straightness of the top. The effect, combined with the use of graduated drawer heights, is to give the façade a sense of lift and upward movement toward the top. The piece, with its large brasses, could have been made any time between 1755 and 1795, although the use of cock-beading on the case around the drawers suggests a date nearer 1780–1795.

A later development is the reverse serpentine (figure 5), sometimes called an "ox-bow front," which is related in movement both to blocked forms and to the serpentine forms that dominate the next period. This chest again has vertical projections and recesses as in figure 4, but without the same break to distinctive units. The movement is that of a gentle outward roll to the handle brasses; the motion then recedes behind the central escutcheon to move out again and terminate on the other side near the end of the drawer; the base molding and the top carry out the same movement, and the legs use the reverse-curve foot but in a looser form than on the blocked piece; the lower edge is a simple loose shape like the movement of the front. The whole composition borders on the placid but is saved by its strength of statement, its large units, and its use of three instead of four

4. Chest of drawers, eastern Massachusetts, 1755–1795. *Courtesy of Israel Sack, Inc., N.Y.C.*

5

6

drawers, allowing for a bigger, simpler area of shaping than would have been possible had the piece been made with the customary four drawers.

The chest of drawers in figure 6 reverses the movement of that in figure 5 and completes the style shift from blocking to the fluidity of serpentine shapes. Starting near the ends of the drawers, this motion moves in behind the brass pulls and out behind the central escutcheons, projecting them toward the viewer. In fact, this is blocking turned inside out, so that it moves in with a rush from the side and then out, making the central part of the façade seem to project beyond the rest of the front although it is actually flush with the corners. The base molding and the top follow the form of the case, and the legs have strong serpentine shapes; the knee brackets, which now move in to follow the inward curve, show a quick, more nervous line with a fretted point or drop, as in figure 4. The brasses, of superb rococo pattern, are Chippendale in style, just as the small, tight, compact, rather square quality of the piece also asserts "Chippendale." It is only in the shaping of the front to a true serpentine form that the subsequent Early Classical Revival period of 1790–1815 is foreshadowed. In this piece features of both periods are superbly united, creating a form with the sturdy, strong, massive quality of the Chippendale period, and the suave movement of façade found in the Early Classical Revival bow-front chest of drawers. The serpentine is so crisply, tightly, strongly drawn that it is one with the stronger, tighter designs of the Chippendale taste.

Figure 7 shows a chest façade with the appearance of more gentle movement. The curve of the

5. Chest of drawers, Rhode Island, probably Newport, 1780–1795. *Courtesy of Israel Sack, Inc., N.Y.C.*

6. Chest of drawers, eastern Massachusetts, probably Boston, 1780–1795. *Courtesy of Israel Sack, Inc., N.Y.C.*

7. Chest of drawers, Pennsylvania, Philadelphia, 1780–1795. *Courtesy of Israel Sack, Inc., N.Y.C.*

8. Chest of drawers, eastern Massachusetts, possibly Boston, 1790–1815. *Courtesy of Israel Sack, Inc., N.Y.C.*

7

8

front seems stretched out and relaxed. The brasses are smaller; paired oval backs hold simple bail pulls, and the escutcheons are simple, oval accents. The movement is more gradual. The serpentine curve no longer begins to roll in from the edge of the drawer; rather, the corners of the case show a broad chamfered or canted corner so that the movement can begin from what appears to be the edge of the piece. The strong, broad chamfered front corners continue down into the bracket feet. The bulkiness of the Chippendale style is still apparent, but the front is serpentined and the top shaped to rounded front corners, as found in so many tables of the Early Classical Revival period.

The full Early Classical Revival façade is achieved in the chest in figure 8. Strong, elegant reverse curves make a lavish movement, and the canted corners are brought to a thinness which correctly responds to the lighter elegance of this new phase; simple oval brasses and straight bracket feet carry out the straight vertical line of the corner posts.

Figure 95 shows the culminating design of the Early Classical Revival serpentine chest of drawers. It lacks canted corners and has been lifted up onto high French bracket feet which provide the final finesse necessary to create a totally new elegance.

These gradual shifts in style have given rise to the term "transitional furniture," for it is often impossible to pinpoint the moment of change from one design attitude to another. Indeed, the most fully developed expression of a new style either encompasses or consciously rejects the old, and is therefore often very much aware of it; frequently a designer skips back one or two styles deliberately for inspiration. The Philadelphia chair in figure 9 has a strong relationship to bannister-back chairs like that in figure 10, a style of fifty to ninety years earlier. New designs are rarely completely new. Again and again throughout the history of design, earlier ideas which are perhaps still in production are rethought and reutilized in a more up-to-date way. Sometimes this updating is not recognized by the maker; he may, in fact, think that he is making something just like the earlier product, but the taste current at the time of actual creation always imbues a design with its own feel-

9

10

ing. It is virtually impossible to make a copy of an earlier piece without adding to it something from one's own time, as we shall see clearly when we come to examine fakes and copies. (A comparable example is seen when we read later translations of earlier literary works. We do not now read Pope's translation of Homer in order to understand Homer, for instance, but in order to understand Pope and his time, to see what he unknowingly added from his own period. Copies, interpretations, translations, always incorporate within them the translator's own beliefs about the earlier objects.)

Figure 11, a bannister-back chair probably made as late as 1800 to 1830, is a striking instance of this. The type first came into fashion in the very early years of the eighteenth century, when bannister backs were massive and richly bold (figures 36 and 37). In the early nineteenth-

century bannister back, we see a tightness and brittleness superbly and crisply executed. The decorative units have a smallness of form—a scattered look, like punctuations across the design. This chair does not have the boldness of early eighteenth-century style, but instead the finickyness—the tight all-over pattern—which we associate with the simpler chairs of the early nineteenth century, particularly those termed "fancy" chairs. This same

9.　Side chair, Pennsylvania, Philadelphia, 1790–1815. *Courtesy of Israel Sack, Inc., N.Y.C.*

10.　Side chair, Connecticut, possibly Fairfield area, 1710–1800. *Yale University Art Gallery; The Mabel Brady Garvan Collection.*

11.　Arm chair, New Hampshire, 1790–1830. *Yale University Art Gallery; The Mabel Brady Garvan Collection.*

conversion of an earlier form into tightly compressed parts is found also in the early nineteenth-century Windsor chair, figure 166.

New designs, the new forms of a new style, were consciously created. They did not, like Topsy, simply grow. The furniture designer-makers consciously created within a design context that they felt to be important, vital, and beautiful. They were often aware of the exact spot in a house where an object would be placed, and they knew it would participate in the panorama of a particular way of life.

The taste of the time dominated. In most cases the cabinetmaker did not violate his material; he used the grain structure of wood logically and sensibly, and he made a piece that would be useful. But he did design the external appearance to meet the prevailing fashion.

11

CHAPTER III

Proportion
&
Organization

12

13

12. Highboy, eastern Massachusetts, 1740–1760. *Courtesy of Israel Sack, Inc., N.Y.C.*

13. Highboy, eastern Massachusetts, 1755–1795. *Courtesy of Israel Sack, Inc., N.Y.C.*

14

15

14. Highboy, Connecticut, 1740–1800. *Courtesy of Israel Sack, Inc., N.Y.C.*

15. Highboy, Connecticut, 1740–1800. *Yale University Art Gallery; The Mabel Brady Garvan Collection.*

Fine furniture did not simply spring out of locally grown or imported logs; instead, it was carefully planned and engineered. It was the conscious creation of men, many of whom were rigidly trained during a strictly programmed apprenticeship in which they learned much beside furniture construction. Again and again one hears the remarks, "What superb proportions—" or "What bad proportions that piece has." The reason is that the designer—the good designer—mastered from others, who had in turn been apprenticed and taught, proportions long known to please the eye. The lesser designers either were not exposed to the best tradition or were unable, because of personal deficiencies, to judge how to use the fine traditions available.

Figures 12 and 13 are typical of many Massachusetts Queen Anne highboys made between 1740 and 1790, and the detailing of both pieces is similar. Alike are the finials, pediments, fan-carved drawers, and the use—above four long drawers—of three drawers in line in the top tier, the center one reaching higher into the pediment. In both highboys the lower case or stand holds one long drawer over three drawers in line, and the skirts are similarly shaped with three simple horizontal cutouts flanked by C-scrolled knee brackets above simple cabriole legs. The feet in figure 13 introduce a difference, however: they have the deep, heavy pad which was used in the second half of the eighteenth century to provide the same mass as claw-and-ball feet.

These two pieces are alike in detail, and, if simply described without real attention to the impact of the design, hard to differentiate. But, despite the similarity, the two pieces make a completely different final statement, which is the result of their different use of proportion. Figure 13, broad in mass, makes one almost wish for the central leg found at the front of a few William and Mary highboys. Its outer brasses are too far to the side, emphasizing the breadth of the front. They are placed directly under the flanking small drawers in the top tier, as in figure 12, but the center shell drawer in figure 13 is broader (unlike figure 12, its outer edges are under the outer limits of the C-shape cutout above), placing the outer brasses toward the side. The whole design of figure 12 is more vertically oriented. Slenderer in design, it makes greater vertical and arching emphasis whenever possible. This is easily seen in the design of the shells, which are compressed and pushed vertically. In figure 12 the distance from the center of the shell to the top is greater than that from the center to the sides. In figure 13, this is reversed. Also, in figure 12 the lower shell is raised further from the skirt so that a vertical emphasis is established even before you reach the arching of the shell, and the recess below is more strongly accented, giving additional vertical thrust.

The same kinds of differences in a subtler form can be seen in the two highboys in figures 14 and 15, both of cherry and both from Connecticut. That in figure 14 is small, narrow, and concise in statement; figure 15, with almost the same details, including brasses, is more open and dispersed.

The artistry of a designer-craftsman depends on his mind, eye, training, and manual dexterity. It is his ability and desire that determine whether he will make a work of art, or a strictly utilitarian object, or something in between. There is, of course, a gradual ascent from the purely utilitarian to the very best, and at each level of sophistication it becomes more a matter of personal taste which of two similar designs is preferred.

The best high-style designers utilized basic, simple proportions which had been known at least since the Renaissance, proportions which are still used by fine furniture designers, such as those in modern Denmark. Such proportions are not difficult to assimilate; they tend to be the simple proportions of 2 × 3, 3 × 4, and the square. That is, given any unit—centimeters, inches, feet, or yards—the proportion 2 × 3 uses two units on one side and three on the other; for 3 × 4, there are three units on one side and four on the other; for a square, each side is of equal length. Combinations of these and other slightly more complex proportions are the fundamental units behind so much of what we prize as beautiful.

Figure 16, a Baltimore sideboard made between 1790 and 1815, has a richly developed façade. The sideboard is one of the most difficult of all forms to achieve successfully, for it is basically a large, heavy rectangular mass poised on toothpick-like legs. To turn this awkward conceit into a graceful object demands the most rigorous and subtle use of fine proportions. The artist who made this piece achieved his success by using a rhythm of squares and ovals. The façade has squared units at either end; one is a door, the other a drawer, and both bow forward from the outer legs to the central section. These outer squares are focused by ovals of flame-pattern veneer surrounded by decorative line inlays, and accented at the center by shining oval brasses. Beginning with the posts, or top part, of the central legs, the central section moves forward and is in the proportions of 1 × 2; the edges of this section are strongly marked by the hortizontal pattern of the zebra-wood veneer on the leg posts. The paired ovals below recall the shape of the outer ovals, but the ovals above, on the long drawer—again centrally accented with shining oval

16. Sideboard, Maryland, probably Baltimore, 1790–1815. *Yale University Art Gallery; The Mabel Brady Garvan Collection.*

brasses—pick up the horizontal movement of the drawer. The middle of the drawer is the central focal point of the design; to mark it strongly, the designer has used the opposite of an oval: a square with incurvate sides. The mass of the case has been subdivided so that attention is paid to smaller parts of the façade, and is carefully patterned so that there are repeats and recalls between various squares and ovals. To break up the horizontality of the case, the zebra-wood panels on the leg posts make a strong slash downward, and this line is carried onto the legs by using the same dimensions for the posts and the top of the leg while the husk inlay carries down the idea of veneer decoration. The strong horizontals are the decorative line oval: around them is veneer, running vertically above and below, and horizontally at either side; the

vertical movement of this veneer is repeated on the front edge of the top. Brilliantly conceived, this great box on spindly legs uses simple basic proportions and a delicate balance of horizontals and verticals to achieve its final elegance.

The great Philadelphia highboy in figure 17 is as carefully integrated as the sideboard, necessarily so since the elaboration could have run to chaos had not everything been carefully planned and executed. Given basic proportions, not unlike other Philadelphia highboys, the cabinetmaker was free, within the prevailing tradition, to create his own statement.

In the center of the skirt a partial shell holds leafage that spills left and right to elaborate the skirt as it moves across to the two C-scroll arches with lambrequin edges; further C-scrolls and leaf-

16

age move across and over the knee brackets; the knee brackets are themselves decorated with leafage that scrolls up onto the knees to lap around the legs as they move toward the feet; the center of the knee is accented with a partial daisy. A second shell decorates the central drawer, recessed and sculptured around a central floral design, repeating the floral motif on the knees; this shell holds leafage that dips to the right and left to curl up around it and move out toward the elaborate brasses. The brasses move in toward the center as they rise, making the whole piece appear leaner than it is. In fact, the piece is almost ungainly in breadth, but the line of the brasses, in and up the center, pinches the waist before flaring out near the top to support the pediment above, like the capital of a column.

The movement of the brass is in part achieved by the choice of the upper small drawer arrangement; the center of the pediment (see detail in figure 18) holds a shell, now larger and pierced to appear lighter, which leans forward at a slight angle; this shell, like the similar one below, holds leafage that moves out to fill all areas of the pediment, lapping over like young plant growth to decorate fluidly all corners and parts of the board; above this, the central finial is shaped and carved to a fourth shell-like form, around a projecting cabochon, and is pierced to lighten the mass. The edge carving of this and the other shell forms is related in movement to the lambrequin carving over the larger C-scrolls of the skirt.

The finial terminates in the only asymmetrical part of the design, a softly curving leafage plume,

17

18

and leans forward at an angle so that if you stand close to the piece to open the drawers you begin to be enclosed by it. On either side of the central finial the cornice of the pediment terminates in floral rosettes, utilizing the floral idea found below in a triangular arrangement, lower on the knees and higher on the central drawer; the line of the cornice moves from the rosettes down reverse curves to the corner plinths, which support flame finials; these finials cap the engaged fluted quarter-columns that outline the front of the upper and lower cases. To unite this incredible piece further, black paint was used as a framing element. Shiny black paint appears on the upper and lower edge of the cornice moldings, on parts of the urn finials,

17. Highboy, Pennsylvania, Philadelphia, 1755–1795. *Yale University Art Gallery; The Mabel Brady Garvan Collection.*

18. Detail of figure 17.

in the flutes of the engaged fluted quarter-columns, on the most projecting part of the mid-molding, and perhaps on the balls of the feet. The scrolls enclosing the pierced part of the pediment shell are black, some of the leafage where it leaves the shell is black, and other areas are painted to strengthen the illusion of recess. A further degree of sophistication is the placement of a slender gilded reed below the upper black molding of the cornice. The gilt picks up the color of the shiny brasses below. (The important role played by brasses can be seen in figure 43, where they are missing from a piece originally designed for them. Brasses were meant to play a major role, and they should be brightly polished.) Carefully considered and superbly executed, the highboy in figure 17 stands as one of the great monuments of furniture design. It shows a sophistication of elaboration seldom achieved in so direct a manner.

Figure 19 is a secretary made by the famous cabinetmaking Goddard and Townsend families, who worked together over many generations, producing some of the greatest sculptured furniture. The Continental baroque style achieved its purest expression in America in the great blocked forms created by these men, the superb bombé pieces of Massachusetts, and such New York pieces as the great card tables in figures 21 and 22. This secretary was created about 1786 for the John Brown House in Providence, Rhode Island, a huge brick mansion built for the opulent merchant-prince who united in his house objects from many parts of the world. His furniture included some of the best Newport work and many pieces (although not all so fine) from Philadelphia.

The lower case of this secretary is a square, and elements of the square as well as more elaborate proportions are used for the upper section.

The front façade is organized to form three strong verticals, established by the blocking and accented by the heavy brasses that move up to the large shells on the slant lid of the desk. The outer shells, like the blocking, are convex; the central shell is concave over the recessed part of the blocking; above these shells, narrower blocking rises to smaller shells carved as below; in the pediment, two double applied plaques bring the movement from the three strong verticals to two units, from which it moves to the central fluted plinth supporting a fluted and corkscrew flame finial; flanking the plinth are floral rosettes which mark the upper point of the cornice of the pediment; the cornice moves down to small plinths supporting similar finials; these finials cap the engaged fluted quarter-columns flanking the bookcase section.

A further degree of sophistication is seen in the placement of the brass button pulls on the slide just above the top drawer. It would seem natural to set these directly over the brass handles of the drawers, but they are placed instead under the

19. Secretary, Rhode Island, Newport, 1755–1795. *Yale University Art Gallery; The Mabel Brady Garvan Collection.*

20. Secretary, Rhode Island, Newport, 1755–1785. *The Rhode Island Historical Society; John Brown House.*

19

outer brass hinges. The hinges had to be that far out in order to give proper support to the fall lid, and if the button pulls had not been placed in conjunction with them their shining edges would have produced an extraneous highlight. By setting the button pulls under the hinges, the artist has created an interesting new area of design.

This is one of the tallest of the nine similar known Goddard-Townsend secretaries. Indeed, many people have the impression (from black-and-white photographs) that it is too tall. But if one studies the actual piece, or a color slide of it, one is immediately aware that the designer recognized this problem: he used light mahogany for most of the surface, but very dark, dense mahogany for the cornice moldings, the rosettes, the moldings that outline the C-shaped cutouts of the pediment either side of the central plinth, the finials, and the engaged fluted quarter-columns. As with the Philadelphia highboy, the whole design is encased, framed, held down and together by the effect of a dark outline around a light mass.

American furniture encompasses a wide variety of expressions achieved by the different regions, or, as they are often called, "style centers." A comparison of this secretary from Newport and the Philadelphia highboy (figure 17) exemplifies the difference between these two centers. Both pieces are of approximately the same date. The secretary is bold, forceful, and baroque in taste; the highboy is more fanciful and elegantly enriched, and comes as near the rococo as America reached before the rococo revival of the mid-nineteenth century.

The secretary in figure 20, also by the Goddard and Townsend families, was made for Joseph Brown, a brother of John Brown and designer of John Brown House. He was a fine amateur architect, designer of several other important Providence buildings, and his secretary introduces some elements not present in other related secretaries. This is the only one with a fourth drawer in the lower section, an extra row of shells, three instead of two double applied plaques on the pediment, and squared platforms under the side finials (as found on some of the tall clock cases and chests-on-chests made by the same men). These changes enrich the front façade and establish three strong verticals that extend from bottom to top with-

20

21

22

21. Gaming table, New York, New York, 1755–1795. *Yale University Art Gallery; The Mabel Brady Garvan Collection.*
22. Gaming table, New York, New York, 1755–1795. *Yale University Art Gallery; The Mabel Brady Garvan Collection.*
23. Arm chair, Pennsylvania, probably Philadelphia, 1730–1760. *Courtesy of Israel Sack, Inc., N.Y.C.*
24. Arm chair, Pennsylvania, probably Philadelphia, 1730–1760. *Courtesy of Israel Sack, Inc., N.Y.C.*

out the movement in toward a surmounting central finial seen in figure 19; instead, the central finial is only one-quarter of an inch higher than those at the sides, and the outer two of the three verticals continue through to the boxes under the side finials. This rearrangement, creating a totally different impact, demonstrates the variety possible in what might be thought of as a rather constraining concept.

Figures 21 and 22 show card tables from New York. They were made at the same time as the Goddard and Townsend secretaries and show the bold movement typical of the American baroque style. That in figure 21 begins in large, massive claw-and-ball feet which move into strong ankles that thrust through the leg into large knees decorated with elaborate asymmetrical leafage; the leafage moves out over scroll-carved knee brackets toward the gadrooning of the lower edge of the

23

24

skirt. Typical of New York, this gadrooning lacks the flute between the projecting elements found in Philadelphia pieces. Above this applied projecting gadrooning, the skirt moves in a strong serpentine form to broad squared corners above the massive knees. The top, following the form of the skirt, is accented at the corner by large recessed squares which held candles; the dished ovals held counters for various games of chance; the remainder of the top is covered with green baize.

Big and bold in form, typical of New York Chippendale-style furniture, this card table emits a very different effect from that of the related table, figure 22, in which the basic elements are similar but the handling of individual parts different. Smaller claw-and-ball feet support slender ankles, which curve gracefully to acanthus-carved leafage with some asymmetrical elements; the carved scrolls on the knee brackets move in a different

direction, away from the skirt, and the projecting molding of the skirt is floral, carved with a different pattern to the left than to the right; above this, vertically grained veneer helps to give a vertical feeling to the deep skirt. The table appears lighter, more elegant, less bold. Together these two very fine but very different expressions of the same basic design show how much the final statement of a piece depended on the ability and desire of the creator.

Figures 23 and 24 form another enlightening comparison. Both these chairs have the same acorn finials, plain turned back posts, arched slats, arms with notched lower edges, baluster-turned arm supports, cabriole legs with chamfered corners and no knee brackets, double baluster and centrally ring-accented front stretchers, sharply tapered rear feet, and the same number of side and rear stretchers. Similar also are the ring accents on the finials,

25

25. Writing-arm Windsor chair, Connecticut, Lisbon, branded by Ebenezer Tracy, 1764–1803. *Yale University Art Gallery; gift of Janet S. Johnson.*

the balusters of the arm supports, and the massive parts of the double baluster-turned front stretchers. The difference is mostly one of scale. Figure 23 is bolder in all its parts. Heavier back posts are connected by deeper arched slats; a heavier skirt is unrelieved by horizontal shaping on its lower edge; massive double baluster and central ring turnings form the front stretcher, connecting massive front legs. The use of striped or tiger maple for the back posts and front seat rails in figure 24 provides a further variation.

How different are the final statements. The chair in figure 23 is bold, forceful, massive, grand, a perfect balance of large-scale and superbly shaped units. The front stretcher alone would deserve display in the finest collection of American design. Starting inside the leg, this stretcher sweeps outward in a curve, then drops to the throat of the baluster; from here it moves out again in a gradual line to the great ball form; then into superbly drawn reel turnings that hold the elegantly slender central ring. Figure 24 is as carefully harmonized, but each part is lighter. It projects a suaver, more elegant image.

Both chairs are very fine; it becomes a personal question which is preferred. Together they show, as do the New York card tables (figures 21 and 22) and the related highboys (figures 12 and 13, and 14 and 15), how different similar pieces can be. The pairs of card tables and highboys are probably each by a different man, so that variations are to be expected; but the chairs are possibly by the same man, who on different occasions chose, for one or more reasons, to make pieces with a quite different impact. It is, then, often a personal choice what kind of impact a designer produces. Just as he was selective in the statement he wished to make, so we should be as consciously aware of what we are viewing.

Figure 25, a writing-arm Windsor by Ebenezer Tracy of Lisbon, Connecticut, demonstrates that a rural object can be as carefully wrought as a high-style object, although the proportions may not be as elaborately developed. The essence of a writing-arm Windsor is the large paddle-like arm projecting to the left, a sizable mass that is both visually and structurally detrimental to the design, since it produces a lopsided effect. In this example, baluster-turned legs of exquisite line support a large chestnut seat; above this, the arm rail flies out to the left, holding below it a drawer that is locked into place by a candle slide, further overbalancing the design. Recognizing the problem inherent in this design, Tracy added counterbalancing; he placed a large drawer below the seat, which functions both as a useful storage area and as a bold mass that helps visually to hold the chair to the floor. And, as a further corrective, he placed the comb of the back one spoke off-center to the right. A brilliant conceit, and a simple answer, of balancing an object pulled out of shape by its function.

As each new style emerged, each region developed its own basic interpretation of the standard forms: chairs, highboys, etc., in any one style center all had similarities but, of course, each designer made his own personal statement within the tradition. Such statement can be seen very clearly in the organization of the highboy in figure 26. Although it was traditional in New England to arrange the drawers of Queen Anne highboys as in figure 12 (that is, with the short drawers in the upper tier), in figure 26 this was not followed, and the basic change has allowed for certain new design possibilities. Beginning at the floor, the cabriole front leg, seen from the front, seems to have just one dimension in width from ankle to knee; but when viewed from the corner, we can see the gradual increase in width as the leg moves to the knee; the actively shaped skirt has a central drop, rather than just flanking drops, a feature typical of Rhode Island pieces. The arrangement of the drawers in the bottom section is the standard design of a long drawer, with three brasses above three short drawers—the center one shallower to leave room for the skirt shaping. But the small central drawer has three brasses, an unusual number for New England. Because of the unusual arrangement in the upper case, this pattern of brasses (three on a long drawer above three on a short central drawer, flanked by those on the small side drawers) is repeated in the upper section; the result allows for a tighter pattern of the brasses below, where they are forced together because the drawers are shallower, to explode apart, to become more dispersed: the same spring and upward thrust as that created by the response between the smaller shell at the bottom of the Philadelphia highboy (figure 17) and its more open, expanded, pierced shell in the pediment. Again and again, this explosion above, this moving upward and outward is used in designing great objects. In the highboy in figure 26, additional vertical lift is achieved by tapering upward the veneer panel which marks the center of the piece. The dark area between the veneer panels of the drawers of the lower section is quite narrow; but starting at the bottom drawer of the upper section is a broad central panel, which decreases drastically as it moves upward from drawer to drawer. This upward taper once again adds to the general movement upward, and one strongly suspects that originally the top of this piece was intended to display fine pieces of silver, pewter, glass, or china.

By the eighteenth century, American furniture had become somewhat removed from its English sources, and to some degree this was a conscious choice. But in the seventeenth century the differences were mostly a matter of the simplification caused by ruralness and a lack of original craftsmen. This is not to say that differences are not observable between the work of rural English and American craftsmen; but, except for the pieces by the best men, such differences are less conspicuous in the seventeenth than in the eighteenth century. The press cupboard in figure 27 has sources in the Midlands of England, where similar turnings and carvings were widely used.[*] The combination of Tudor roses (on the central lower panel) and thistles (at the bottom of the lower side panels) was very common in England, symbolizing the unity of England and Scotland under James I. This press cupboard is one of the better seventeenth-century American pieces and shows the beginnings of original American thinking. There is the same sturdiness as in English work, but England lacked maple, a factor which to a great degree conditioned the difference between American and English country furniture. Dramatically shaped turnings such as those flanking the upper central panel could be executed in maple, whereas they would be more difficult in the woods commonly used in English country work. These little pieces of turned wood have a clarity of statement

* John T. Kirk: *Connecticut Furniture, Seventeenth and Eighteenth Centuries* (Hartford, Conn.: Wadsworth Atheneum; 1967), pp. xii, xiii.

which is as superb as any in the history of furniture design.

The front façade of the press cupboard is organized to use units of twos, threes, and fours; at the base three panels, with flat floral carving, are flanked and divided by four applied split spindles (created by turning a whole piece and then cutting it in half and attaching the flat side to the main surface). Above the split spindles are applied heart forms. The drawer section, one long drawer masked to look like two, is composed of octagonal units punctuated at the center with wooden pulls flanked by applied oval bosses, which rake to move the design upward; these octagonal panels in turn are divided and flanked by triglyphs. A central emphasis has been established by making the lower central panel a different shape from the two flanking panels, and by surmounting it with the strong pattern of the central triglyphs; above the drawer, dentils rake outward from the center toward the bold ring- and baluster-turned columns which, though vertically oriented, have strong horizontal movement in their deep rings. The upper section of the cupboard, recessed to give play between the upper and lower units, has flanking panels elaborately decorated with applied bosses and intruding points. Between these two paneled doors is the focal point of the design: the central panel has a different mode of decoration from the rest of the piece. It is divided into a five-part design, each part focused by a demi-cylinder; flanking the central panel are paired split balusters of superb drawing; the bases of these turnings have the same shape as the applied bosses on the flanking panels and the drawer; above is a reel turning, then an upward tapering to a narrow reel-shaped neck, then a large demi-cylinder—like the demi-cylinders on the central panel—and finally the third reel, capped by a button top. Above the recessed area a projecting section repeats the balance of the drawer, two long panels with central accents; these panels are divided and flanked by three plaques, carved in tulip patterns, repeating both the triple motif and the flat tulip carving found below. The cupboard is further accented by black paint used on the applied bosses, split spindles, and columns; the molded edges of the panels in the upper section are painted yellow-white under zigzag black lines. Originally a riot of color

26. Highboy, Rhode Island, 1730–1750. *Yale University Art Gallery; The Mabel Brady Garvan Collection.*

26

27

27. Press cupboard, Connecticut, Wethersfield-Hartford area, 1670–1710. *Yale University Art Gallery; gift of Charles Betts.*

28. Chest over drawer, Connecticut Valley, probably Hadley area, 1670–1710. *Yale University Art Gallery; The Mabel Brady Garvan Collection.*

29. Chest over drawer, Connecticut Valley, probably Hadley area, 1670–1710. *Yale University Art Gallery; The Mabel Brady Garvan Collection.*

28

29

30

and an extravaganza of pattern, this piece is carefully, almost painfully, organized. It reveals, as few documents can, the seventeenth-century passion for pattern and color.

Surprisingly little furniture is known from the beginning of the seventeenth century. But, as in other art forms, there was a great flowering in furniture design at the end of the century. At the very time when England was moving on to the more elaborate, court work inspired by the return of Charles II, when a taste for plush and elegance, lightness and curves was developing, America, too, experienced a new degree of elegance; but it utilized as its sources the more elaborate versions of England's late sixteenth and early seventeenth centuries, which it had already handled in simpler ways.

Paint played a major role in seventeenth-century furniture. One of the most famous of the late seventeenth-century forms is known as the "Hadley chest." (Over 150 similar pieces were found in the Hadley, Massachusetts, area, although it is now known that they were also made further south in Connecticut.) The basic units of the decoration are a scroll, a tulip, and two types of leaves; and three of these units are evident in the flanking panels of the chest over drawer in figure 28. The design begins at the bottom of the panel with a scroll, moves up to a tulip turned sideways, then branches to a leaf design with a serrated edge; in the central panel is the fourth unit of design, a smooth-edged leaf flanking the central star. Most of these chests over drawers have lost their original polychrome decoration. In many cases time has worn the paint away, and some pieces have been repainted in an overall color. But in most instances, as in figure 28, they have been industriously refinished by collectors who want their objects to look like wood. This effect was not part of the original intention of the designer-cabinetmaker, however. By removing the original paint,

30. Tall case clock, New Jersey, works by Isaac Brokaw, "Bridge Town," 1790–1815. *Courtesy of Israel Sack, Inc., N.Y.C.*

31. Card table, probably Rhode Island, 1790–1815. *Courtesy of Israel Sack, Inc., N.Y.C.*

the intention of the maker—the very person the collector supposedly respects—is falsified; the designer, in fact, is not allowed to have his original statement preserved. His use of paint, his method of deliberately organizing the façade, is stripped away; and only part of what he sought to achieve remains. One is left with "Early American" in the most vulgar sense. Fortunately, the designer's original intention is to a great degree preserved in the chest over drawer in figure 29. Figure 28 now looks like an all-over textile design with a pattern bordering on chaos, instead of the order in figure 29, which is the essence of all good design. In figure 29 one sees purposeful placement, rhythm, and pattern. The vertical side posts, the vertical stiles between the panels, and the drawer were originally painted black on the outer surface of the two-plane carving. The outer surfaces of the other areas were painted red and the recessed part of the carving possibly yellow, although it is now difficult to be certain. This use of black paint to organize the façade into strong verticals and horizontals is far from an isolated example. It recalls the use of black paint on the Philadelphia highboy (figure 17), where the paint was used as a frame and as a means to articulate the decoration further. The same type of make-up, or cosmetics, is present on the Goddard and Townsend secretary (figure 19), where dark mahogany surrounds and frames the light mahogany of the case. The half-round moldings of the William and Mary desk in figure 74 are painted black, intensifying their framing effect. And the clock in figure 30 is another of the many pieces that use black paint; further, as with the Philadelphia highboy, it uses gold on moldings and columns to enrich its decorative appeal. The probably Rhode Island card table in figure 31 uses black accents on the edges of the top, above the legs in the flutes of the inlay, and on the outer edges of the front faces of the legs, but it achieves this darkness not with paint but by burning the wood dark with a hot tool.

All this furniture was consciously created. It was as carefully planned to make a particular impact as the training and skill of the individual craftsman allowed. And just as the creator was conscious of his actions, the viewer must understand the elements brought into play to create each piece, if it is not to remain simply a functional object.

31

CHAPTER IV

The Role
of
Small Details

32   33

The preceding chapters have stressed the effect of balance in design, how it is achieved, and the kind of impact different sorts of balance can have. Small details, such as the baluster turnings on the upper section of the press cupboard, in figure 27, were seen to be of major importance. Often it is these details that make one piece better than another, just as it is sometimes the balance of the larger parts or masses that adds the ultimate mark of distinction.

The William and Mary period, that echo of the baroque style, established in America for all time the awareness of the movement from bold to slender, the interaction between areas of different scale, and the curve. One of the richest forms to develop at this time was the bannister-back chair (see figure 32). The spindles for the back were created by turning units similar to those that formed the side posts above the seat; these were then split in half and placed with their flat side forward (the same procedure was used in making the applied split spindles for the case pieces of the preceding period). Figures 32 to 35 show chairs typical of those made in the Boston area during the first quarter of the eighteenth century. Elegant and tall, they are the American answer to the high cane-back chairs of England, the Lowlands, and France. Their tall elegant backs served as a backdrop to the elaborate clothing of their owners, and the great arched crests fanned behind the elaborate wigs of the period.

These four chairs, although similar, show subtle variations which produce major differences in their quality. The tops of the front legs, above the block that holds the front stretcher, are different on each chair. In figure 32 the lower turning is a ring supporting a baluster form, above which is a reel form with a partial reel above. The shape and arrangement of these units creates a visual lift

32. Side chair, eastern Massachusetts, possibly Boston, 1700–1735. *Yale University Art Gallery; The Mabel Brady Garvan Collection.*

33. Side chair, eastern Massachusetts, possibly Boston, 1700–1735. *Yale University Art Gallery; The Mabel Brady Garvan Collection.*

from the squared block below. The main form, the baluster, moves out and in and out again; in the lower reel turning there is a scooping in, then out; then with the upper reel the leg moves into the seat frame. It is precarious, it is poised, and it is exquisite. It has that same fragile construction seen in the highboys of the period, where the case is poised on weakly constructed legs (figure 68).

In figure 33, the units are more complex and more difficult to read because of their compactness. There is a ring, supporting a baluster, supporting a reel, supporting a ring, then a reel and a partial reel. It is too complicated, too difficult to read, without being complex enough to add an exquisite involvement. The result is in fact heavy and inelegant. In figure 34, the forms are dissolved and bland and read as a series of heavy masses. In figure 35, a different kind of seat construction eliminates the turned area because the rails are housed into the top of the front legs instead of the seat frame resting on the legs.

Other differences between these chairs can be seen in the spacing of the four split balusters. In figure 33 they are placed closer to the center, creating the feeling of a central panel as in the contemporary caned or leather-paneled chairs, whereas in figure 32 they are more evenly spaced across the back. The double baluster and ring-turned front stretchers, too, show a marked difference; that of figure 35 eliminates the central ring to produce a more English turning by placing the balusters on either side of a central reel.

Bannister-back arm chairs have a design problem which does not arise in side chairs. In side chairs the silhouettes of the split spindles can exactly repeat the side posts. On arm chairs the area of the back posts where the arms are attached is usually left as large as possible, and on the chairs that have square parts in the posts (as in figures 36 and 37), rather than rounded posts (as in figure 38), it would be detrimental to the design to preserve this squareness when making the split balusters. Therefore, this area must be designed differently. Figures 36 and 37 solve the problem in two different ways. Above the level of the arms the split spindles of figure 36 are the same as the side posts, but from the arms downward they sim-

34. Side chair, eastern Massachusetts, possibly Boston, 1700–1735. *Yale University Art Gallery; The Mabel Brady Garvan Collection.*

35. Side chair, eastern Massachusetts, possibly Boston, 1700–1735. *Yale University Art Gallery; The Mabel Brady Garvan Collection.*

34

35

36

37

ply wobble tremulously. In figure 37 the designer
has been more creative; he has introduced a different element of design into the bottom third of the
split spindles; he has used the baluster and reel
combination on the front legs just below the arms,
but he has compressed the baluster form so that it
is like those lower on the front legs. He has also
used a fifth spindle, which carries the central accent of the ring of the front stretcher up through
the back to the center of the crest rail.

On the other kind of bannister-back chair, with
no squared parts, the area where the arm joins the
back posts is still a problem. In figure 38 the
designer has used, for the lower half of the split
spindles, the baluster form under the front of the
arms and the reel turning above the tapered turn-

ing of the back posts—which he did not repeat at
the top of the split spindles.

These differences, although subtle, are often the
distinction between a great and a mediocre piece.
One of the most famous names in American furniture design is that of Samuel McIntire, who
worked in Salem, Massachusetts, at the end of the
eighteenth and the beginning of the nineteenth
century as a house architect, furniture designer,
and carver. The two sofas in figures 39 and 40 are
possibly carved by him, or at least both seem to be
by the same carver and have the quality associated
with McIntire. There are, however, major design
differences: the front legs in figure 40 are reeded
and an exposed seat rail and a loose cushion are
used; figure 39 has smooth legs and a seat uphol-

36. Arm chair, eastern Massachusetts, possibly Boston, 1700–1735. *The Metropolitan Museum of Art; gift of Mrs. Russell Sage.*

37. Arm chair, eastern Massachusetts, possibly Boston area, 1700–1735. *The Metropolitan Museum of Art; gift of Mrs. Russell Sage.*

38. Child's high chair, New England, possibly Little Compton area, Rhode Island, 1710–1800. *Yale University Art Gallery; The Mabel Brady Garvan Collection.*

38

stered over the rail. But a study of the three panels that form the crest rail is the most enlightening area of comparison. In the sofa in figure 39, the central rectangular plaque carries a basket with its front edge tipped upward to produce an arched line as the top of the basket; this line continues to the right and left in serpentined leafage that moves gracefully toward the inner tips of the swags on either side panel; the swags dip to support fruit, and after curving up again terminate in pendant drapery. Starting at the end and moving across, there is a swag, a serpentine line, a central arch, a serpentine, and then a swag; together these form a graceful flowing line. In figure 40 the central basket pitches forward; at either side of it there are swags with the same downward curve,

39

40

and this dip is repeated on the side panels in the swags. Beginning from one end, there is simply a series of semicircular movements that scallop their way across the top rail; there is little flow, only staccato rhythm. The quality of the carving on both sofas is superb, but the designs chosen separate the two into different degrees of excellence.

Another famous name in American furniture design is that of Duncan Phyfe, of New York, who worked at about the same time as McIntire. The side chair in figure 41 is possibly from his workshop, for it shows the fine attention to detail which is typical of his work. The chair is designed to have one continuous flowing line from the top of the crest rail, down the back post, and across the seat rail to terminate above the front leg. This basic line relates the chair to its Greek source. As the wood moves down, the width of the top surface increases, reaching its greatest breadth over the front leg. On Phyfe-quality pieces the reeding that decorates this top surface also expands in width as it flows downward and out; on lesser examples it maintains one width, so that by the time it reaches the front leg there is a flat part on either side of it, as in figure 42.

Phyfe also paid extraordinary attention to his selection of woods, as did other cabinetmakers of equal excellence. In figure 41 the recessed panel of the crest rail, the recessed oval plaque of the midrail, and the rectangular panels on the upper face of each front leg are veneered with branch mahogany. A mahogany chair was inlaid with patterned mahogany so that there was further richness at the main focal points. Detailing like this was what raised already fine designs to an even higher level.

The role that brasses played in organizing a façade to achieve a vertical thrust and careful organization has already been mentioned. Brasses were highly polished, and to achieve greater effect some were gilded or silvered. They not only united the lower and upper decorative areas but also served as highlights in candlelit rooms. Indeed, at night they were the most prominent part of a piece, and the modern fad for leaving brasses dirty or even purchasing already permanently dirtied brasses borders on the absurd.

The chests-on-chests in figures 43 and 44 were probably made by the Dunlap family in New

39. Sofa, Massachusetts, Salem, 1790–1815. *Yale University Art Gallery; The Mabel Brady Garvan Collection.*

40. Sofa, Massachusetts, Salem, 1790–1815. *Yale University Art Gallery; The Mabel Brady Garvan Collection.*

41

Hampshire in the latter part of the eighteenth or the early part of the nineteenth century. That in figure 43 is incomplete; it never had brasses, not even later pulls. Perhaps the customer was waiting to acquire the money to pay for the imported ornaments, for brasses were almost always imported until after the Revolution—and even well into the nineteenth century. This superb chest-on-chest retains its original peach-pink paint, now faded to a softer hue. At the base can be seen the typical Dunlap use of exquisitely shaped short cabriole legs with deep C-scrolled knee brackets, fan patterns (which really look as if they have textile on the outer part and openwork between the ribs), paired S-scrolls, and a molding that the Dunlaps called "flowered ogee." In the cornice the flowered ogee appears again above bold dentils. Between these two very decorative areas there is now a blandness. Had the design been completed with

the expected brasses, the lower and upper areas of decoration would have been joined, as in figure 44.

Each of the major American style centers had its own interpretation of a style. Although the chief difference is that between their overall design approaches, part of what makes the distinction is their particular way of handling small details. Figures 45 and 46 show the crest rails and upper part of the splats of two Chippendale chairs made between 1755 and 1795, the first in Massachusetts and the second in Philadelphia. As with the classical carvings of the sofas (figures 39 and 40),

41. Side chair, New York, New York, 1810–1820. *Yale University Art Gallery; The Mabel Brady Garvan Collection.*

42. Side chair, New York, New York, 1810–1820. *Yale University Art Gallery; The Mabel Brady Garvan Collection.*

42

these two chairs show a marked difference in treating similar ideas. In the Massachusetts chair, the ears have a slightly swelling center and simple serpentine ends; the crest rail moves from the ears to the central shell, which is small and neatly carved; under the shell, the crest rail divides and continues into the strapwork of the splat; the area where the straps start is at first filled, and the fill decorated with triple chip carving; the outer straps terminate in small scrolls that rest upon inner straps, which have joined each other and then move outward in a tight circular movement to twist in upon themselves; they again touch, then separate to terminate in tight scrolls as found above. Below, this scrolling is supported by the lower part of the splat, which is divided from it by a carved line; this line delineates the upper straps and makes a visual break between the upper and lower parts.

The chair from Philadelphia (figure 46) has boldly knuckled ears with a swelling center which rises above the raised and scrolled outer edges. The bulging center has chip-carved decoration; the crest rail moves under the shell without any visual sign of strapwork; instead of finding the shell on the upper edge of the strapwork, as a separate unit, it is placed on its front face, and is larger and bolder, more convex and fluidly carved than the Massachusetts example. The outer strapwork of the splat begins below the crest rail and drops and scrolls in upon itself very much as in the Massachusetts chair; the central area, however, has separate straps that act as links to the lower ones, which have risen from the shoe on the rear seat rail (for the full splat, see figure 113). In the Philadelphia example there is a flow of scrolls from the crest to the seat rail without a break into an upper and lower part. The Philadelphia chair is

43

43. Chest-on-chest, New Hampshire, 1768–
1800. *Yale University Art Gallery; The
Mabel Brady Garvan Collection.*

44. Chest-on-chest, New Hampshire, 1768–
1800. *The Currier Gallery of Art.*

44

45

fluid, while that from Massachusetts is more brittle and tightly drawn. The variations are the result of different artistic approaches to the same basic vocabulary.

The difference in design attitude can be seen again in the treatment of the carving for the knees of two chairs from the same two regions. The sharpness of the knee on the Massachusetts chair (figure 47) continues down from the sharp corner of the seat rail above; the leaf carving is tight in design and flat, linear, and begrudgingly bestowed; it appears from under the seat rail to cover the surface, much like a thin layer of hair. In the Philadelphia example (figure 48), the roundness

of the corner of the seat frame is carried down onto the rounded knee, creating a richer movement than the sharp ridge on the Massachusetts example; the carving is lush and fluid like the carving in the pediment of the Philadelphia highboy (figure

45. Detail, side chair, eastern Massachusetts, possibly Boston, 1755–1795. *Yale University Art Gallery; The Mabel Brady Garvan Collection.*

46. Detail, side chair, Pennsylvania, Philadelphia, 1755–1795. *Yale University Art Gallery; The Mabel Brady Garvan Collection.*

46

17). From a scroll at the base of the knee bracket, leafage grows up toward the seat rail, and from there moves out again to flowing acanthus that laps around and down the leg toward the foot. The carving is deeper than in the Massachusetts chair, and it is richer and laid on with a greater sense of motion. Each region has its own way of handling details. Once again it is a matter of personal choice which is preferred.

Given that a piece of furniture is of fine proportions, excellent execution, and superior quality, it is often the details that raise the object of the level of art. This, however, is not always the basis of quality, for many superb simple, undecorated pieces exist. Nor does it follow that a whole object is necessarily successful because certain parts are good. But craftsmen who had the skill to produce such details usually made fine pieces, unless they were merely specialists in carving, inlay, or some other limited profession. Of course, such fine detailing also depended on the customer's willingness to pay for the necessary time. Fortunately, it was the rule that the better designers usually obtained the patronage of those able to pay for fine work and sophisticated enough to appreciate it. Those customers with a good eye for line, form, and pattern are generally ready to patronize the artists who can produce such refinements.

47

47. Detail, side chair, eastern Massachusetts, probably Boston, 1755–1795. *Yale University Art Gallery; The Mabel Brady Garvan Collection.*

48. Detail, side chair, Pennsylvania, Philadelphia, 1755–1795. *Courtesy of Israel Sack, Inc., N.Y.C.*

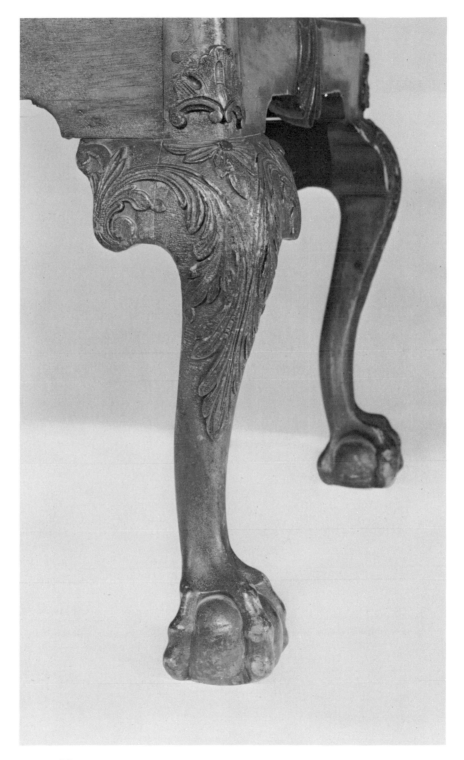

48

CHAPTER V

The

Interpretation

of

Sources

49

49. Chest, Connecticut Valley, Hartford, Connecticut, to Hatfield, Massachusetts, 1670–1710. *Courtesy of The Henry Ford Museum, Dearborn, Michigan.*

The act of creation involved in designing furniture usually includes a conscious borrowing or rejection of a previously created form, as I have stressed. For American designers the earlier form, if foreign, was usually English; but these borrowed forms were invariably simplified for a provincial setting.

During the colonial period, America was far removed both geographically and intellectually from the major artistic centers of the world. Reactions of early visitors suggest that Boston, New York, Newport, Philadelphia, and Charleston were so stylish that they seemed almost like parts of London, but other observers have implied more accurately that such comments show an overzealous desire to appreciate what was happening in America. The term "provincial" not only designates a setting with a less elaborate culture, but also describes a state of mind in which two quite separate attitudes are confused. The colonists wanted to see themselves as set apart—even, to a degree, better. Yet, at the same time, they wanted to consider themselves no different from the Londoners or people they revered as culturally correct. Benjamin Franklin with his coonskin cap set himself apart from sophisticated Europe but paradoxically thought of himself as the same. Dissimilarities were present from the very beginning and the settlers knew they were inevitably distinct from England; but England was still home—the mother country and the source of so much that made life meaningful. The difference lay basically in a new way of thinking. By the onset of the Revolution, a crucial minority was ready for a final break with England. The thought behind the break, which had been developing for years, the new sense of liberty which allowed seventeenth-century New England only a handful of offenses punishable by death whereas England retained hundreds, this new insight into mankind, had an effect on the objects men made and used. A clear example—though a later one—of the effect of political and religious rethinking upon objects is found in nineteenth-century Shaker design. Here a reassessment of the whole meaning and pattern of life gave rise to simplified furniture. To achieve this, the Shakers used eighteenth- and early nineteenth-century forms, ladderbacks and turned and square-legged tables, but simplified them to express beauty in undecorated things. A comparable rethinking, although far less conscious, seems to have been part of what made American furniture different from its English antecedents.

Not only did the political setting differ, but the social setting was simpler and in many cases the cabinetmakers were less well trained, less skilled in elaborate detailing. These cabinetmakers, although they sometimes advertised themselves as having worked for kings and lords, were not, on the whole, the men who had made the elaborate English pieces. Instead, they knew simpler designs appropriate for simpler people.

That the difference was both conscious and unconscious is illustrated by John Adams's famous remark, "My sons ought to study mathematics and philosophy, geography, natural history, and naval architecture, navigation, commerce, and agriculture, in order to give their children the right to study painting, poetry, music, architecture, statuary, tapestry, and porcelain." For Adams, painting and even porcelain were self-conscious arts that would flower only in the more sophisticated stages of a culture; and he did not include silver and furniture design. Clearly these genres, the only American art forms until long after the Revolution to be judged great by world standards, were unconscious arts like agriculture. They were already a natural part of life, fully integrated into daily existence. Their makers did not continually feel inadequate, as the painters did, and this freedom, this unself-consciousness allowed the flowering of a great expression.

England's great furniture is its court work. Exquisitely designed and balanced to a rich ornateness, with involved carving and pattern, it was well suited to the large aristocratic houses of England, where it was combined with court dress and elaborate silver, in a patterned, totally aristocratic environment. To have produced that type of design in America would have been as inappropriate as copying Buckingham Palace for the home of the first President of the United States. Economically, socially, and politically it would simply have been unreasonable. The court work, therefore, was not the source of American furniture design. It was neither emulated nor often imported, being far too expensive and unsympathetic, both in scale and appearance.

The majority of the American immigrants were people of lesser means. Many came from the lower classes, and they created here, so far as they could, the kind of context they had known before. If they had lived in a simple house with a dirt floor, it was not surprising that they should do so here. If they had had extremely simple, rustic furniture in the Old World, it is not surprising that they sought simple furniture in the New. The parallel must have been extremely obvious at the time. A man of more considerable means, such as John Winthrop, first Governor of Massachusetts, when he sent for his wife, asked her to bring their household goods so as to continue life at the same level he had known before.

Thus America's chief sources for furniture design were the designs of the lesser cabinetmakers of London and the cabinetmakers of the provinces. The inspiration in the mid-eighteenth century, for example, was not Chippendale's pattern book with its elaborate designs but the furniture that already existed: actual simple English objects. American craftsmen rarely went to source books until about 1790; instead, they borrowed from the objects they or their teachers had known in England or that were imported.

Some of the variations in American furniture are the result of the presence here of certain woods not available in England. These new materials acted hand in hand with other differences to reinforce the streamlining of designs. By the middle of the seventeenth century, Massachusetts settlers had found and were using broad, strong, but light pine boards, which differed from the softer deal of England, as well as maple, which is not indigenous to England.

Following English precedent, the first chests made in America were of oak. Some had paneled tops, copying a practice prevalent in England, where wide oak boards were difficult to obtain because much of the English oak had been burned earlier to make charcoal. Soon, however, pine six-board chests (a name given to those chests with just a top, bottom, front, back, and ends) emerged here in great profusion, for they could be made simply by nailing or dovetailing together the available wide boards. This change in construction changed the type of decoration used. On paneled pieces the decoration was necessarily focused within the small areas or units created by the panels, stiles, and rails, as in figure 29. On chests made of large boards, such as that in figure 49, there was a new large area for decoration, and the design would range over the entire front. This opening up of design was a major step toward what was to become American furniture's personal statement.

The abundance of maple in the United States was equally important; it could be turned to a slender elegance not as readily achieved in oak, walnut, or the other woods available in rural England. Oak has a very visible grain; walnut does not have the wiry strength of maple; and yew, elm, and ash all have similar handicaps. Maple allowed for exquisite turnings like those on the press cupboard (figure 27), and for the slender, raking, elegant legs on Windsor chairs (like those in figure 142). Beech, which can be turned somewhat like maple, was available in both countries. But its quality never affected the English designs as maple did the American, and Americans never used it in quantity since maple had greater design potential.

A few of the cabinetmakers—Thomas Affleck of Philadelphia, for example—did make London-type furniture when they first arrived in the colonies,

50. Upholstered side chair, England, possibly London, 1730–1740. *The Victoria and Albert Museum.*

51. Upholstered side chair, Pennsylvania, Philadelphia, 1740–1760. *Yale University Art Gallery; The Mabel Brady Garvan Collection.*

51

but they shifted within a very short time to an American approach to design. Although such men knew how to make more elaborate, up-to-date English objects, it is clear that they deliberately chose to work in the American idiom, either for personal reasons or because of the purchaser's preference. The colonial product thus became a completely new statement as a result of the factors of distance, thought, earlier training, and the materials available in the new setting.

The upholstered side chair, or "back stool," in figure 50 is one of the great English high-style expressions in wood. The back and seat are upholstered in ornate, original needlework, and the wood areas are equally rich and elegantly handled. Masks on the knees are enclosed in leafage that joins the paw feet through hair-carved ankles to make one cascade of deeply carved elaboration. This chair expresses England's highest achievement in furniture between 1730 and 1740. The carving has dissolved the basic form by elaborating it to a high level of artistic achievement. Typically, if one took away the carved element there would be virtually no cabriole form; there would be only the backing of the carving. The great French pieces dissolved the form to an even greater degree, making the entire leg one grand elaboration; even the backing was dissolved. This approach to design was not used in America, however, until the mid-nineteenth century.

The Philadelphia back stool in figure 51 typifies elegant American furniture of the period. It displays a simpler original needlework textile of American or English origin; the rear of the back is covered in watered moreen of a muted yellow. The seat is not deeply upholstered. From under its slender edge move graceful cabriole front legs, which are simple in their movement and reflect the rather straight quality of the Irish taste that so heavily conditioned Philadelphia products from 1730 to 1750. The decoration of the front legs consists of simple C-scrolls that support or underlie the knee movement, and trifid feet that terminate them at the base. The cabriole form is intact, and the whole design depends for its elegance on the graceful movement of a simple line: the simple curves of the back, seat, and legs are picked up in the movement of the flat stretchers. The English chair embodies elaborate elegance; the American,

52. Secretary, Massachusetts, Boston area, 1730–1750. *Courtesy of Museum of Fine Arts, Boston; M. and M. Karolik Collection.*

53. Secretary, eastern Massachusetts, 1730–1760. *Courtesy of Israel Sack, Inc., N.Y.C.*

52   53

54

54. Secretary, Connecticut Valley, Hartford, Connecticut, to Springfield, Massachusetts, 1755–1800. *Mr. and Mrs. Charles L. Bybee.*

55. Side chair, Rhode Island, probably Newport, 1740–1760. *Museum of Art, Rhode Island School of Design.*

56. Side chair, England, 1710–1730. *Present location unknown.*

elegant simplicity. One presents full elaboration; the other uses it as an enhancement. Both are magnificent, but both achieve very different effects intended for their different contexts. Indeed, this is just the kind of English product that was not the source for American work. Instead, American craftsmen borrowed from simpler, often weaker English designs, and managed to create a new kind of elegance from them.

Some comparisons between American pieces and their sources follow. But, first, figures 52 and 53 demonstrate the difference between an "English" piece made in America and a truly American design. The famous Massachusetts Queen Anne secretary (figure 52) is close enough to English work to be considered almost an English expression. This anglophile piece was probably produced by a person who had either just arrived in the colonies and not yet learned the American idiom, or who tailored his work to suit a buyer

55

56

with English tastes. The piece is, so far as we know, unique; for this reason, it does not teach us as much about the development of American design as the second secretary in figure 53. The latter is simpler and just as handsome, deserving perhaps to be called "starkly elegant" rather than "simple." The elegance of the lines of the bonnet and the arched, fielded, paneled doors are here more evident and immediate. The whole is stripped of elaborate veneers and the American idiom appears clearly.

A different American expression can be seen in more rural pieces. In figure 54 this different taste is expressed in the direct pattern of juxtaposed rectangles: the paneled doors, the slant lid, and the drawer fronts. The mass is supported on an undulating-shaped skirt, typical of the mid-Connecticut Valley, held on short cabriole legs with club feet. The design is very suitable for a small Connecticut Valley house. Its directness,

starkness, and simple arrangement of well-defined and well-proportioned rectangles, and, in particular, its superb surface of aged maple with traces of the original red paint, make this one of the great examples of American country furniture. Figures 53 and 54, then, demonstrate the American expression in two entirely different traditions.

The distinction between American furniture and its English equivalent is often subtle. The Rhode Island Queen Anne chair in figure 55, made of local maple, utilizes each line, each area of movement, to create a simple harmony without excess. Slender, and therefore appearing tall and narrow, the rounded back posts rise to rolled shoulders. These move into a scooped crest rail above a splat with simple ears, from which the lines drop in long reverse curves to the seat; simple reverse-curve knee brackets move toward reverse-curve cabriole legs with well-proportioned club feet. The curves are completely harmonized, ex-

57

58

cept for the stretchers, which contradict this movement and are perhaps one of New England's major design failures.

The English chair in figure 56 is a comparable piece that attempts very much the same thing, again in a simple manner. But in comparison with the American chair it introduces too many breaks in the flow of the lines: the area where the back posts join the crest rail drops in small notches, a carryover from Chinese design; the splat has straight downward breaks at its neck; the waist of the splat narrows too much, then flares out to small curves, from which the splat drops straight again to the reverse curves just above the shoe. The front knees and knee brackets seem heavy against the lightness of the seat rail. On the other hand, it is a relief to have no stretchers, and, although awkward to the American eye, a cabriole rear leg does give a sense of movement that is missing from the chamfered back posts of figure 55. However, although the cabriole rear leg does relate to the front leg, and gives a sense of unity to the base of the chair, it has little design relationship to the upper part of the back post such as is found on the American example. These chairs show two different ways of expressing simple movement, but the American one projects a slender, simple beauty not present in the English piece.

The Massachusetts dressing table in figure 57 illustrates American elegance in the Early Classical Revival period, and stands in direct contrast to a related English design (see the sideboard in figure 58). In the American piece, a rectangular mass is organized to form a simple bowed front. This front holds two squared drawers on either side of one long rectangular drawer, above an arched skirt; the bowing produces a simple elegance of thin-skinned, taut movement typical of the period; lift and elegant poise are provided by the upward movement of the tapered feet and by the arched cutout of the skirt, which again echoes the bowed front in movement. The arched cutout raises up the case to make the space enclosed by the front legs and skirt seem light and open, and as important to the design as the wood area. The front façade is enriched on the side drawers by arched flame veneer, and on the center drawer by a matched flaming veneer, which gives further arching and lift; these veneers are closed in by crossbanded veneer with light areas that flicker across the face (as in figure 125); the bottom of the skirt has a delicate, decorative line edging that con-

57. Dressing table, eastern central New England, possibly Boston, 1790–1815. *Museum of Art, Rhode Island School of Design.*

58. Sideboard, England, 1780–1800. *Courtesy, City Art Museum of St. Louis.*

59

59. Chest, England, 1600–1700. *The Victoria and Albert Museum.*

60. Chest, Connecticut, Wethersfield area, dated 1714. *Courtesy, Henry Francis du Pont Winterthur Museum.*

tinues above the square-tapered legs, which in turn are enriched with delicate husk drops that carry the decoration downward; the legs narrow to light and dark cuffs, whence the feet taper sharply toward the floor, a New England feature. In comparison, the similar English piece has sturdiness, weight, and settled forms. It lacks the exquisite line and balance of the American derivative.

The seventeenth-century English framed chest, figure 59, is the type of piece that was the source of inspiration for a group of furniture made in the Wethersfield, Connecticut, area, represented by figure 60. The Connecticut chest, of board construction, has been decorated with patterned stamps similar to those with which leather is decorated. The decorator had stamps of at least three designs. The first was in the shape of a half-circle, with which he made C-shapes; by using this once and then reversing it, he could also make the circles and the S-shapes. The second had a set of small dots that, joined together, made the lines. A third was a star which he made with the initials S D and the date, 1714. Using this stamp method, he divided his front façade into three vertical panels like the English chest with its elaborately decorated stiles, and used similar large diamonds with paired curves at their points and petaled patterns at their center.

Another simplification was the transferral of marquetry patterns into paint. The English late sixteenth- or early seventeenth-century wainscot chair in figure 61 is one of countless pieces of English furniture inlayed with a two-handled vase

60

or earth motif that holds one or more central flowers (usually either a pink, as here, or roses) and flanking tendril vines, sometimes, as here, supporting birds. This decoration was used on chairs, cupboards, chests, beds, and virtually all forms, each inlayer using his own interpretation of the basic idea. Figure 62 shows a chest of drawers which, like others from the Saybrook-Guilford area of Connecticut, used a painted version of the marquetry pattern, which provided a similar colorful enrichment by an infinitely easier method: the middle long drawer has a two-handled vase, a pink, and birds.

The simplification of decoration techniques was not confined to the American interpretations of European sources; it occurred within the colonies as well. Figure 63, a tall case clock from the Reading area, is an example of Pennsylvania's use of marquetry. In the door various woods shaped to floral and leafage patterns rise from an earth motif, and floral vines decorate the bonnet; the corner posts of the mid- and lower sections are floral-carved (the feet and finial are not original). The tall case clock in figure 64 is from the same area of Pennsylvania but has an inlay of white and pink wax on both doors and the lower panel. This would be a somewhat easier method of setting in color to provide the same flat, multicolored effect and may have been a German tradition. The simpler tall case clock in figure 65 achieves its decoration by the use of paint. The waist door shows a cup holding flowers and a sunburst, flanked on the waist of the clock by tendril vines similar to those carved in the engaged quarter-columns on the preceding clocks; on the door of the bonnet, around the glass face, is a tendril vine similar to those inlayed in wax. The case and decoration were simple to achieve, and yet the decorative effect is even more pronounced than that made by the more complicated methods.

61. Arm chair, England, Midlands area, 1600–1650. *The Victoria and Albert Museum.*

62. Chest of drawers, Connecticut, Saybrook-Guilford area, 1670–1710. *Courtesy, Wadsworth Atheneum, Hartford.*

62

63. Tall case clock, Pennsylvania, Reading area, works by Asabel Cheney, East Hartford, Connecticut (probably not original to case), 1790–1815. *Yale University Art Gallery; The Mabel Brady Garvan Collection.*

64. Tall case clock, Pennsylvania, Reading area, works by Benjamin Witman, Reading; case dated 1801. *Yale University Art Gallery; The Mabel Brady Garvan Collection.*

65. Tall case clock, central Pennsylvania, 1800–1850. *Philadelphia Museum of Art; Titus C. Geesey Collection.* (The painted decoration was removed after this photograph was taken.)

63

64

65

Simplification from carving to paint was not the invention of Americans but it did, here as elsewhere, become a major means of decorating inexpensively great quantities of furniture, particularly in the early nineteenth century. This nineteenth-century crop of painted ware became known as "fancy furniture." The eagle in the back of figure 66 is beautifully carved and is the distinctive feature of this early nineteenth-century chair from New York. The quality of the eagle, which is better than the rest of the chair, suggests that it may have been purchased by the chairmaker from a carver who specialized in such parts. A related design is achieved in the chair in figure 67 by painting an eagle in gold and brown on a shaped pierced surface. This eagle would have been infinitely quicker to create, particularly if a stencil was used, and is as decorative. These simpler pieces made available to a broad cross-section of the population a plenitude of inexpensive attractive objects.

The way in which cabinetmakers used decorative details to condition the final impact of a piece has already been dwelt on, but many times entire surfaces were overlayed with patterned paint to make a piece of simple wood look as if it was made of elaborately grained material (the painting process itself was called "graining"). Many of the pieces that were painted have been stripped and their nakedness revealed (this barbaric removal of the original surface was mentioned in Chapter III) but some unharmed pieces are included here to demonstrate the makers' original concepts.

The William and Mary highboy, figure 68, is veneered with burl maple, which gives the tight all-over pattern fashionable in France and then in England. This type of veneer was made by sawing a burled growth into thin sheets, a process which was time-consuming and therefore not inexpen-

66. Side chair, New York, New York, 1810–1820. *Yale University Art Gallery; The Mabel Brady Garvan Collection.*

67. Side chair, American, possibly Connecticut, 1810–1840. *Old Sturbridge Village photograph.*

68. Highboy, Massachusetts, Boston area, 1700–1735. *Yale University Art Gallery; The Mabel Brady Garvan Collection.*

67

69

69. Chest over drawers, eastern Massachusetts, 1700–1720. *Yale University Art Gallery; The Mabel Brady Garvan Collection.*

70. Highboy, Connecticut, probably southeastern area, 1740–1760. *New Haven Colony Historical Society.*

sive. The chest over drawers, figure 69, has used paint to elaborate its surface in much the same way. The real and pseudo drawer fronts have elaborate S-shaped stenciled "panels," and the ends of the case are covered with multiple squiggly lines, enriching them to burl-like, tight designs. Both the burled and the painted pieces are splendid expressions of much the same idea, but they stand within two separate traditions. Both achieve an all-over rich, tightly ornamented surface in the finest way their traditions allowed.

The Connecticut highboy, figure 70, is made of maple, and is painted a pinky orange and grained with black to simulate the elaborate veneering of more "developed" pieces. Although at first glance the pattern seems somewhat haphazard, there is a careful repetition of similar decoration on similar areas. The drawers of the upper case have a matched pattern and the painter has been careful not to polarize the movement; that is, not everything that is angled goes in the same direction. In the center of each long drawer there is an oval: the one on the top drawer slants to the left, the one on the second drawer to the right; on the boards that separate the drawers of the upper case, the diagonal lines have different directions. This alternation of movement keeps the eye from traveling just one direction and thus away from the piece. It retains the movement within the design.

Pieces made later in the eighteenth century, and in the nineteenth, were often painted to appear exactly like complexly grained wood. Endless simple pieces were made to look like rosewood or fancy mahogany. The chest of drawers in figure 71 is an example. Written in pencil under the top drawer is: "Made by E. Morse/Livermore/[Maine] June 7th 1814." Not only are the drawers grained, but they and the edges of the top are painted to a decorative line usually achieved by patterned inlay or "stringing." Another nineteenth-century piece, figure 72, is of a slightly later style, about 1820 to 1840, when rosewood and marble were fashionable. This stand is inscribed by Philip H. Saunders of Danders, near Salem, Massachusetts. By using paint he achieved a "marble" dropleaf not attainable, in America, in real marble. With paint, something new has been added!

70

Not all painted decoration imitated a real material; very quickly it was used also to achieve abstract patterns that elaborated the surface as they had done early in the eighteenth century (figure 69), but expressing a new freedom and delight in colorful enrichment. The stand in figure 73 has "sponge" decoration that makes circular patterns on the top, rail, and drawer, and tiger-maple patterns on the legs.

Figures 74, 75, and 76 form an interesting comparison, since each piece uses a tiger-maple pattern in a different way. The desk and stand imitate it; and the highboy (of real tiger maple), uses its pattern as a background for simulating walnut or mahogany grain. The desk is of tulip poplar, except for its lid, which is hickory, a denser, harder wood probably thought necessary for this more actively used part. The surface has been decorated with paint to represent patterned maple, and the half-round moldings are black to intensify their enclosure of spaces. It is a simple country piece with sides that continue down to form the legs; but despite its simplicity it has been elaborated to present a more opulent and interesting appearance.

The stand in figure 75 was made about a century later than the desk; it is inscribed in pencil, under a drawer: "Made by B. F. Rollins, March, 1818," and is thought to be from Camden, Maine. Light and simple in form, it is much like the piece in figure 73 but with an extra drawer, wooden knobs, shaped top, and paint imitating a real wood rather than a fanciful expression.

Many people today would say that the highboy in figure 76 "gilds the lily." This incredibly sophisticated piece from Salem, Massachusetts, is made of maple with tiger-maple drawer fronts, a wood that is one of the hardest to bring to a smooth surface (it tends to pockmark as the plane picks out the small bits that form the pattern). To work it correctly demands the sharpest plane and the most careful attention. On the surface is the original painted graining, which simulates walnut or mahogany. The fans are painted with subtle colors to form arched rainbows, and the drawer fronts around them have little design so as not to interfere. Although extraordinary today, this use of tiger maple behind painted graining was fairly common in New England at the end of the eight-

71. Chest of drawers, Maine, Livermore, inscribed "Made by E. Morse/Livermore/ June 7th 1814." *Courtesy of The Henry Ford Museum, Dearborn, Michigan.*

72. Dropleaf stand, Massachusetts, inscribed, "P[hilip] H Saunders/Mill St Danders, " 1820–1840. *Courtesy of The Henry Ford Museum, Dearborn, Michigan.*

73. Stand, New England, 1790–1830. *Old Sturbridge Village photograph.*

71

72

73

74

75

eenth and beginning of the nineteenth century, for the pattern of the wood gave life and richness to the painted decoration. It added a greater sense of depth than is found with similar decoration placed upon an unpatterned wood. It is not clear why a cabinetmaker capable of this level of design did not use veneer; but he has achieved, by the painted method, a fine feeling of clarity, a sharpness of outline, a distinction of form, and a swiftness of motion that is unexcelled in American furniture design. The legs alone would place this piece in the first rank of furniture sculpture.

Paint was thus used to organize a façade, enrich a surface, and simulate more elaborately patterned woods. It was also used in combination with special short-cuts, or easy methods, to obtain a more complex visual experience than the amount of work involved might seem to dictate. As we have seen, there are two basic ways to build a case piece: frame construction and board construction (figures 59 and 60). The cabinetmaker who made

the press cupboard, figure 77, in the Hampton area of southern New Hampshire (1700 to 1740), quickly achieved his piece by nailing together a series of boards, making a drawer, and hanging the doors on cotter-pin hinges; the sides are simple boards shaped to continue at the base to form legs, and the top is a simple board with a slanting edge. But to make the piece more pretentious—akin to the complicated paneled press cupboards of the previous century, such as that in figure 27—he applied moldings to the edges of the front boards and then painted them black. No structural value was gained; the piece is no sturdier than it was

74. Desk, Connecticut, 1700–1720. *Courtesy of Paul Koda.*

75. Stand, Maine?, possibly Camden, inscribed "Made by B. F. Rollins, March, 1818." *Old Sturbridge Village photograph.*

76. Highboy, Massachusetts, Salem, 1740–1760. *Yale University Art Gallery; The Mabel Brady Garvan Collection.*

76

77

78

before these decorative moldings were applied; but a sense of weight and force has been added so that the piece takes on an aura of grander construction. Over the rest of the front façade, which is of tiger maple, small squiggly lines have been painted to add additional surface movement and relate the panels to the burled veneer found on many contemporary pieces. Further decoration has been introduced in pictorial forms: on the lower section a central tree is flanked by scrolled leafage on the outer panels: the initials of the original owner, Sarah Rowell, appear on the drawer (her name is painted in full across the top), flanked by leafage vines; and the pine sides are decorated with squiggly lines around grand, open, moving lines that form plant tendrils, with a bird making the focal point.

The chest over drawer in figure 78 looks like a framed chest, but it is in fact a simple six-board chest with a drawer. It is enriched on the front by thin strips of wood arranged to appear like the heavy stiles and rails of frame construction, and the centers of the pseudo panels are accented with applied bosses, like the panels on the ends of the press cupboard in figure 27. To emphasize the paneled effect further, the chest is painted red and the raised areas black. The maker has achieved an elaborate visual effect very simply. He has made a mock façade, and we have a delightfully enriched six-board chest with the surface play usually achieved by more complex construction.

Taste is, therefore, the most commanding force behind design, but the furniture makers, while creating stylish exteriors in a variety of ways, always produced useful, serviceable objects. Pieces were carefully planned to have what the maker felt to be (sometimes correctly and sometimes incorrectly) fine proportions; he then elaborated the design, maintaining an interesting tension between the verticals and the horizontals, organizing the masses so that they balanced, making parts light or heavy to produce boldness or elegance, and drawing the eye toward the focal point. To provide unity and enrichment, colored woods or paints were often used. Attention was paid to each small detail, and different regions placed their own peculiar accent on a standard vocabulary. Each maker sought to achieve the finest that he could in the time allowed.

77. Press cupboard, New Hampshire, Hampton area, 1700–1740. *Yale University Art Gallery; The Mabel Brady Garvan Collection.*

78. Chest over drawer, Connecticut, south-central area, 1670–1710. *Yale University Art Gallery; The Mabel Brady Garvan Collection.*

CHAPTER VI

~~~~~~~~~

High-Style,
Country,
Primitive,
&
Rustic

W hat are the different types of American furniture? What differences distinguish the elaborate from the simpler pieces?

American furniture is normally lumped together into one classification: "Early American." But, as in American painting, there are various levels or kinds of expression—separate genres that evoke separate responses and experiences. Paintings by John Singleton Copley and Joseph Badger are expected to be very different. The artists were very different men, with diverse training and skills. Copley's paintings glorified people of Boston and New York, many of whom lived lavishly and sought to emulate the latest mode as directed by elaborate London taste. Badger's paintings made a simpler, although not necessarily a less involved, statement. Furniture, too, makes different statements.

European furniture is generally divided into various strata or layers (the court work at the top, the folk or peasant art at the bottom), and of each very different things are expected. What makes a piece great in Paris is not the same element sought in a piece from the provinces.

We have seen that Americans borrowed their designs from English country furniture, and that the various style centers in America expressed English designs in different ways, with varying ideas of design, movement, and pattern. So far, we have discussed this chiefly in terms of the high-style centers: Boston, Newport, Philadelphia, New York, and Charleston. But we have yet to see the attitude to design developed in the American provinces: in such places as Connecticut, Vermont, New Hampshire, Maine, the interior of Virginia, and central and western Pennsylvania.

To understand American furniture, it is necessary to see that the styles as they evolved over the years—from early to late seventeenth century, to William and Mary, Queen Anne, and Chippendale, from Chippendale to the early classical designs and onward—did not do so in one continuous line. Rather, it was a many-layered affair. In the top layer—where the styles changed rapidly, where Europe was *the* source, *the* inspiration for change—are the major "high-style" centers; these centers contained the majority of the best-trained cabinetmakers, men who knew the European modes as a result of having trained there themselves or associated with European-trained cabinetmakers or their products. These were the sophisticated stylists, the people who set the tastes by reflecting European ideas while changing them into an idiom suited to the American context. These were the men who made the superbly balanced pieces, whose designs incorporated the traditionally good proportions and details. They understood that a perfect tension can create that balance which brings a design to the point where it captures the beholder, and they could do this so skillfully that the viewer is still unaware of how it is achieved, of all that is involved. They could create elegant simplicity by the supreme art of making order out of chaos. These were the craftsmen who made the great Philadelphia highboys and the Goddard and Townsend secretaries.

It must be remembered that these highly skilled men were not always called upon to make a fully elaborated piece, however. Each area of decoration cost more, and some purchasers, whether because of personal taste or economics, desired pieces without the fullest elaboration. Therefore, the man who made the elegant chest-on-chest in figure 79 might also have been called upon to produce that in figure 80. Both have the finest proportions and are well executed; the latter simply lacks the elaborate pediment area and the complex brasses. Thus, the *work* of these craftsmen must be divided into two subgroups, which I shall call "elaborate high-style" and "plain high-style."

In the second layer of furniture makers are the men who often worked in provincial cultural centers, generally with less sophisticated training. They made what might be considered the high-style of the rural areas. In some cases, they had been trained in high-style centers and were capable of making high-style objects, but again because of personal choice or the power of the purchaser's taste and purse they made objects which were akin to the provincial setting in which they lived. Such a man was Eliphalet Chapin, who, for approximately three years, worked in Philadelphia and then returned to East Windsor, Connecticut, to make pieces like the great chair, figure 114, so different from its Philadelphia counterpart, figure 113. These rural men, on the whole, reinterpreted American high-style designs rather than European. That is, they worked second-hand from European inspiration; sometimes they created simpler, and sometimes more complex, designs than one would find in a high-style center. If they developed a simple line it was not generally the powerful, springy line of a high-style center, but instead a more languid, soft, gentle line. If it was a complicated line, it was generally a stronger, more complex one; for example, in Connecticut a powerful, tight, springy line co-existed with a languid, open elegance; what is missing there is suave, sophisticated movement and development.

At this level a highly personal design attitude was created by rethinking designs from American high-style centers and introducing into them a strong streak of individuality—an individuality always appropriate to the context in which the ob-

79

79. Chest-on-chest (high-style), Pennsylvania, Philadelphia, 1780–1795. *Yale University Art Gallery; The Mabel Brady Garvan Collection.*

80

80. Chest-on-chest (high-style), Pennsylvania,
Philadelphia, 1780–1795. *Yale University
Art Gallery; The Mabel Brady Garvan Col-
lection.*

81

81. Chest-on-chest (country), Connecticut, East
Granby area, dated 1802. *Yale University
Art Gallery; The Mabel Brady Garvan Col-
lection.*

82. Chest-on-chest (primitive), Pennsylvania,
1755–1800. *Yale University Art Gallery;
The Mabel Brady Garvan Collection.*

jects were to be used. The resulting group of
pieces was as revealing of the way of life of its
area as the high-style pieces were of theirs. Both
were the best of their region; the difference was
that the style of life was not the same—the milieu
in which they existed was different. It is difficult
to label this group, since it is not a lesser one so
much as a separate one. Because these pieces are
from rural settings they are called here "country"
pieces. Such words as "provincial" and "regional"
were considered but discarded: "provincial" is
now a derogatory term, and "regional" could as
well include high-style centers.

The third level in this complex development is
what might best be called "primitive." This group
of pieces emerged from a different European background and is part of the folk-art tradition. It does
not simply emulate high-style or country designs;
rather, it uses a different means of expressing
what is fashionable, and for it different things
constituted "fashion." The high-style maker
looked to Europe for inspiration; the country cabinetmaker looked to the high-style domestic cabinetmaker; the primitive cabinetmaker was to a
much greater degree removed from the tradition of
either. As well as having his own tradition, he
borrowed from both high-style and country designs; but he always added the originality that
comes from feeling free to work eclectically within
certain customary limits.

In many cases this group of furniture appears
more original than the high-style designs, for it
often combines many styles within one piece, as
did, sometimes, country furniture. A chair might
have a William and Mary base, a Queen Anne
splat, and a Chippendale crest rail. Such combin-
ing of elements is often credited to a style lag (the
time it takes a new style completely to condition
the work of a provincial craftsman), but this is an
oversimplification. Many chairs made as late as
1800 or after incorporate all the styles of 1700 to
1800, and by then all but the most isolated makers
could have known what constituted a total Chippendale, or 1755–1795, expression. The designer
of primitive furniture was likely simply to update
the most prominent or most conspicuous part. Almost all chairs that incorporate two styles have the
latest displayed in the most prominent area,
usually the crest rail. Another aspect of "primi-

tive" individuality is the updating of parts that were most easily changed. In the chair in figure 115, for example, the back carries the pierced splat and eared crest rail of the Chippendale period, while the base continues a William and Mary pattern of some fifty years earlier. Had the maker been creating a complete Chippendale expression he would have had to carve cabriole legs and claw-and-ball feet, instead of using simple lathe-turned legs with quickly carved Spanish feet. The time he saved would dramatically affect the cost.

This mixture of styles is part of what makes primitive pieces appear original and inventive. Indeed, they are in a sense more original, since they were often designed to suit specific requirements or as an expeditious way of producing a piece rather than, as in high-style designs, to ape the European taste. Nonetheless, the façades were usually still made to be fashionable—within the purchaser's concept of that word—while the interior received the custom-made design. In primitive furniture there seems to be a greater lightness of touch, almost a sense of humor; it is more intriguing, more eccentric, more patterned; and it often depends upon its surface quality to make it delightful. These are the pieces that cannot aesthetically survive refinishing; the pieces that must retain their original paint, be it elaborate graining, a simple blue paint that has faded and changed to a marvelous blue-green, or reds that have changed to mixtures of red, orange, pink, and brown. A good rule of thumb to keep in mind about primitive objects is that they will usually be painted, whereas high-style or country pieces usually utilize the grain of the wood instead. In part, this is because primitive cabinetmakers had less access to the "finer" woods and less money to buy elaborately grained wood; but, more important, these paint-decorated surfaces suited the context, the milieu for which the furniture was made.

High-style and country furniture represented the most sophisticated and expensive work by the most elaborately trained men of their respective areas. Primitive furniture was less expensive, and it was made, in general, for a different social stratum; it was therefore used everywhere, in the simpler homes of the city as well as the country. Sometimes it was also found in sophisticated town homes, although usually in the lesser rooms. I

82

83

83. Highboy, (high-style), Pennsylvania, Philadelphia, labeled by William Savery, 1755–1788. *Courtesy of Israel Sack, Inc., N.Y.C.*

84. Highboy (country), Connecticut, East Windsor, 1771–1807. *Yale University Art Gallery; The Mabel Brady Garvan Collection.*

have described it here as a third group, which may seem to place it below country. But that is unfair. It is more accurately a second level under both high-style and country, whichever is ascendant in a given locality.

The fourth level of furniture expression I have termed "rustic." It covers those pieces that are simply joined together in the most rudimentary fashion. A taste for these rudimentary forms was consciously and highly developed in the Adirondack furniture of the early twentieth century, for grottos and other consciously rusticated settings. The term is used here, however, to designate pieces made by untrained men who had a need and fulfilled it in the best way they could. It was primarily useful furniture, without a strong conscious effort for beauty, but it often achieved great charm. Although unskilled in the art of cabinetmaking, the makers usually wished to be surrounded by attractive objects and frequently spent considerable effort on the things they needed. A half log held up on four sticks, or indeed on three, serves as well to support a person as an elaborately executed walnut bench; it is more rudimentary but not necessarily less attractive. In this group the whimsy, inventiveness, and patina of a piece is highly prized. We should value its color, its wear —perhaps the carved initials of various owners— its integrity, and its forthrightness, for it seems similar in these qualities to its pioneer makers and users. Examples of rustic furniture are very difficult to find, for such pieces were not valued by their owners; they were something to replace as soon as possible. It is also the hardest group to date or regionalize, since it does not reflect any style that would suggest a time of creation, nor does it usually have any features that relate it to regional developments.

Not all American furniture falls easily into these four categories, but the labels do serve to separate it into more easily understood groups. Figures 79 to 139 are arranged to demonstrate the basic characteristics of the four groups or attitudes toward furniture design. The chest-on-chest in figure 79 is as carefully organized as the Philadelphia highboy, figure 17. The bottom case holds three long drawers flanked by engaged fluted quarter-columns over ogee bracket feet; the upper case holds four long drawers below three short drawers in line, flanked by engaged fluted quarter-columns. The pediment, including the frieze, is a separate unit placed on top of the upper case of drawers; the frieze is carved to elaborate fretwork below a dentiled cornice that supports a broken-arch pediment, its cornice terminating in leaf-carved rosettes; the pediment is pierced to curved lattice work, which rises at the center to support a floral basket; at the front corners are square dies that support finials turned to a ring, reel, flattened ball, and an elongated neck supporting carved flames. Large in scale, elaborately and exquisitely delineated, with each element superbly made and organized to rise to an elaborate pediment, this piece would have been placed in a room with imported damask, china, and mirrors to help complete the setting for a formal, elegant way of life. The bedroom that would have housed it may have served as well as a place to eat and receive guests for tea, and for other elaborately patterned ceremonies. It is a high-style piece by a fine designer-craftsman who worked rather strictly within the highest aesthetic tradition.

The chest-on-chest in figure 80 is similar. It is as finely organized, with the same use of superb proportions. But it makes a different statement. It is similar in that the three long drawers of the lower case are flanked by engaged fluted quarter-columns above ogee bracket feet, and the upper case holds four long drawers below three short drawers in line, flanked by engaged fluted quarter-columns. The differences are first that the chest-on-chest in 80 does not have an elaborate pediment but instead a bold cornice decorated simply with dentils; second, a local Pennsylvania walnut was used instead of imported, elaborately patterned mahogany; and third, simpler brasses are employed. These brasses suggest a later date—although this is not necessarily so. A late feature was also used in figure 79: the cock-beaded rather than lipped drawers and the urn-like side finials suggest the Classical Revival period.

The two pieces are equally refined in proportion and in their handling of detail; the main difference is that figure 80 is less elaborate. They are so alike in design and quality that they could be the work of the same man or workshop. On the other hand, the plainer one may be the result of a cabinetmaker's inability to provide an elaborate pediment.

84

Many independent carvers were available, however, to provide carving for cabinetmakers who either did not themselves have the skill or the desire to carve. More likely, then, it was a question of the purchaser's desire not to spend additional money on elaboration, or simply his desire to have a plainer piece. The similarities, not only of detailing but of basic design approach, place both pieces in the same group, figure 79 in elaborate high-style and figure 80 in plain high-style.

As the engraved oval silver plaque above the top drawer testifies, the country Connecticut chest-on-chest in figure 81 was made for Hannah Forward in 1802. It tells us many things about country cabinet work: first by its date and second by its general attitude toward design. In Philadelphia by 1802 this piece would have appeared old-fashioned, although it could have been ordered there by someone preferring a familiar style or wishing to match furniture purchased at an earlier time. In Connecticut, however, which was removed from continual contact with England, pieces such as this were not inappropriately behind the times. The late features include the use of oval brasses, both for pulls and lock escutcheons, and the urn-shaped finials. The rest of the features are Chippendale in style. Although the chest-on-chest in figure 79 has similar late features, the impact of country Connecticut design is totally different. Here the high-reaching elegance is lacking. Part of the difference is created by the drawer arrangement. In the base there are four long drawers, instead of three, which produces a stronger horizontal orientation; and the upper case holds five long drawers instead of having the upper tier broken into three short drawers, which would have helped to push the action vertically. The piercing of the pediment forms C-shapes that, although more ornate, are frozen in their movement. In the Philadelphia chest-on-chest the flowing line of the top molding is followed by one direction of the lattice work; in the other direction the lattice work curves toward the central finial, and the small units echo the dentils below; the whole pediment achieves an elegant interrelation of movement and motifs. On the Connecticut piece the central cartouche has an intriguing shape, but it has no flamboyant upward- and outward-reaching motion; it is flanked by cornice scrolls that mount higher and

terminate in small, statically carved sunburst rosettes that, being higher, push the central finial downward. The side finials are interesting forms but lack the great swelling movement of the Philadelphia ones. This is indubitably a country piece, made for a country setting by a country cabinetmaker who, like the Philadelphia maker, was satisfying the needs and taste of his particular area.

The primitive chest-on-chest in figure 82 is a composite individual statement by a man who misunderstood the traditional means of organizing the front façades of such pieces: it combines the designs traditionally used for highboys and chests-on-chests. The bottom case holds one long drawer below five short drawers, the center one carved to a central shell holding leafage (usually chests-on-chests within the high-style or country traditions were organized to three or four long drawers); the upper case holds four long drawers below five short drawers, arranged similarly to those in the lower case; the pediment is carved to a central shell below pinwheel rosettes. The designer has not only used a highboy arrangement for the short drawers, but has used it incorrectly. In the lower case he has placed a short central drawer carved with a shell flanked by leafage as in a Philadelphia highboy, but he has placed it over rather than under the long drawer. Either this is a misunderstanding of the highboy design, or in producing this chest-on-chest the designer felt that the decorative area should not be next to the floor but raised slightly and placed under the mid-molding. He has repeated the arrangement of the five small drawers in the upper case, but without expanding it to give the sense of upward movement found on high-style highboys. Also, in the high-style tradition, if there is a shell on the pediment, there is usually not one on the drawer immediately below; and if there is one in the pediment, it holds leafage which spills out to fill the flat area to either side. A further primitive conceit is the movement of the leafage. Instead of being light and elaborately arranged, it is in simple S-curves studded with leaves.

Still another unsophisticated feature of this primitive chest-on-chest is the arrangement of the brasses. On the lower drawer, these are close together as on the long drawers above; just above, they move out and around the lower shell drawer, and back in again to the waist of the piece; this makes for a circular movement rather than an uplifting one as in high-style pieces. (The feet and the finial plinths are restored. The piece would have been improved if the feet were given the same strong, vertical movement as those in figure 79.) This cabinetmaker is clearly outside the two traditions that produced the great Philadelphia highboy and the Chapin highboy, figure 84. Instead, he has made a piece that we can appreciate as a primitive, or as folk art, for it has the power and majesty often found in this great tradition. It would have decorated appropriately one of the simpler Pennsylvania stone houses with white-plastered interior walls—in either the city or the country. It has the same rugged, direct solidity.

The serenely beautiful Philadelphia highboy in figure 83 is labeled by William Savery. In every way it qualifies as high-style, although not all of Savery's work does, demonstrating that a maker can work within more than one tradition depending on his audience. This highboy has the finest proportions and detailing and makes an enlightening statement when compared with one of the country pieces by Eliphalet Chapin.

The country highboy in figure 84 was undoubtedly made by Eliphalet Chapin, the East Windsor, Connecticut, cabinetmaker who spent about three years in Philadelphia. The shaping of the skirt is identical in movement to that of figure 17; the drawer arrangement in the lower case is also similar—the bottom tier is made up of three drawers, with the deeper one at the center, carved to a shell, or in this case a typical New England fan. The upper case shows a simplified drawer arrangement of four long drawers crowned by three deep ones, the central one carved to a more elaborately moving shell than below; this case, like the lower case, is flanked by engaged fluted quarter-columns and crowned by a molding supporting a pediment. The

85. Highboy finial (country), Connecticut, East Windsor, 1771–1807. *Courtesy, Wadsworth Atheneum, Hartford.*

85

86

87

86. Chest-on-chest (high-style), Rhode Island, Newport, 1755–1795. *Yale University Art Gallery; The Mabel Brady Garvan Collection.*

87. Chest-on-chest (country), Connecticut, Norwich area, 1755–1810. *Yale University Art Gallery; The Mabel Brady Garvan Collection.*

Chapin piece resembles not only the Savery piece but also the Philadelphia chest-on-chest, figure 79; all three have a straight molding supporting the pediment and top arched moldings terminating in leaf-carved rosettes. But Chapin's carving is simpler in movement and execution; the strapwork of the pierced pediment moves in toward the central plinth, which projects in a half-cylinder as in the Savery piece. The side finials are turned to much the same form as on the Philadelphia chest-on-chest (a reel turning, supporting a flattened ball with a long neck) but in the Connecticut piece they terminate in a turned button instead of a carved flame. The Eliphalet Chapin piece recalls Philadelphia to an amazing degree, but if made there it would have been out of scale and inappropriately designed. Chapin produced something suited to his own region and he used cherry, a wood highly favored by Connecticut (so much so that it was imported from upper New York State when walnut or other American woods, or even mahogany, could have been obtained).

A closer comparison between the pediment of the Philadelphia highboy (figure 18) and a Chapin finial (figure 85, taken from a different Chapin highboy) reveals the difference between the two traditions. The movement of the leaf carving in the Philadelphia pediment is light, flowing, intertwined, and reaches out to fill all the available areas; it is light like young plant growth. The pediment shell is exquisitely, carefully, and precisely delineated; rich undulating edges are refined by incised lines that also serve to elaborate them; deeper carving moves into black painted C-scrolls that encompass the central shell-like design; the central finial above is rich in pattern and balances four C-scrolls; the outer edge repeats the movement of the shell below; and finally, the cartouche acts as a support to full-blown plume-like leafage that terminates the design. The whole makes up a rich, tightly organized movement and pattern.

The Connecticut finial, on the other hand, is virtually *art nouveau* in its design—shapes that almost, but not quite, touch. It is far more abstract in its movement and countermovement than the Philadelphia example. Most of the design is a counteraction of eight generally C-shaped concave, leaf-like units: the lower two flank the base; five

form the central action; and the main rounded member moves from the base to the left and back to the right to scroll into an additional concave leaf that supports five concave, rounded petals. The result is a beautiful balance that just hints at the haphazard, rather than the complete statement of the Philadelphia pediment.

At present there is no known precedent for the Chapin finial. It may be that this is one of those rare simplifications that produces a genuinely original design. By removing all excess, depending solely upon simplicity of line, a country designer sometimes arrived at something that can be considered wholly new.

Whereas Philadelphia provided the inspiration for many Connecticut designs, some areas of Connecticut, particularly New London County, relied heavily upon the work of Rhode Island, especially of Newport. Cabinetmakers from that eastern county of Connecticut must have apprenticed in Newport, or had contact with work originating there. Both groups used the famous enrichment of heavy blocking and shell-carved decoration, although each used it in its own way.

The chest-on-chest in figure 86 has typical Newport ogee bracket feet supporting a case holding four long drawers; as in most Rhode Island pieces, the mid-molding is attached to the upper case and encloses the lower; the upper case holds three long drawers under two drawers in line, below a pediment paneled with paired applied plaques in typical Rhode Island manner. The pediment has a beautifully arched cornice molding— C-shaped cutouts with molded edges rising to a central fluted plinth supporting a ball and partially fluted urn finial with an acorn terminal. Behind is a closed bonnet. Small brasses rise up the lower case to be set in slightly on the upper case, moving farther in toward the center as they reach the small drawers. These bring the eye toward the paired applied plaques, which then move it in and up again to the central finial. The wood employed is mahogany, and the piece is an elegant statement of the plain high-style group.

The Norwich-area country chest-on-chest, figure 87, seems at first glance almost too close to the Newport tradition to be differentiated from it. Reverse-curve bracket feet support a lower case with four long drawers; the upper case holds three

88

88. Chest-on-chest (high-style), Rhode Island, Newport, 1755–1795. *Norman Herreshoff.*

89. Chest-on-chest (country), Connecticut, Norwich area, 1755–1810. *Courtesy of Israel Sack, Inc., N.Y.C.*

long drawers below an arrangement of five short drawers; the brasses are small and inset toward the center in the upper section; the pediment holds paired applied plaques below a broken arch pediment; above, C-shaped cutouts with edge moldings join a fluted plinth flanked by small baluster turnings. Crowning the center is an urn and corkscrew finial, which is repeated at either front corner on fluted dies. The difference between the final statement of this and the high-style Newport piece is, however, immense. Many factors are involved. In figure 87 the design feels stretched upward, and the piece is, in fact, taller. Instead of the more sophisticated imported mahogany, tiger maple has been used. It is so arranged that the pattern on the bottom drawer rakes to the left; on the second drawer it goes vertically; on the third drawer it rakes to the right; on the fourth drawer to the left; on the bottom of the upper section it is basically vertical, then moves back and forth until it becomes perfectly straight again to reach upward in the paired applied plaques. The whole arrangement is carefully controlled so that the eye moves back and forth up the piece. Had all the stripes been placed vertically, the piece would have taken on a zebra-like quality; had they all been placed to the right or the left, the eye would have moved away from the design as it followed the action of the lines. The brasses are small and do not disturb the surface. At the top, the drawer arrangement makes the loose central sunburst, typical of one kind of Connecticut work, act as a central focus; and the undulating, scalloped outline of the sunburst provides the shape for the central drop below the bottom molding. The bonnet is not closed behind—which helps to eliminate the flat two-plane quality of the Rhode Island example, as it allows the eye to penetrate through and behind the rising pediment. The loosely turned flame finials, now painted a medium dark green, were originally the light moss green discernible underneath and still showing on the small baluster turnings at either side of the fluted plinth. Lower-waisted, with far more enrichment and activity, this piece is in the finest country tradition. It is, in fact, one of the great statements of American design, although it stands removed from the Newport tradition and twice removed from the English. Its expression is new and personal—personal to the cabinetmaker and to the region that produced it and him.

The Newport chest-on-chest, figure 88, made for John Brown's mansion in Providence, is as elaborately conceived as his secretary (figure 19). Strong, reverse-curve bracket feet are edged with blocked knee brackets that, in typical Newport manner, flow down to terminate in small scrolls near the floor—a Rhode Island conceit known also on a few related Connecticut pieces. The four drawers of the lower case are vertically oriented by bold blocking crowned with positive and negative shells, and the case is flanked by engaged fluted quarter-columns. The upper case, with four long drawers under two drawers in line, is flanked by engaged fluted quarter-columns. The whole is crowned by paired applied plaques below a closed bonnet, with floral rosettes on either side of a fluted plinth holding a reeded urn and corkscrew-flame finial. (When this photograph was taken the left and central plinths had been reversed, and the one in the center was turned one-quarter to the left, hiding the flutes of the front face.) The drawers of the lower case are enclosed with cock beading applied to the case; the upper drawers are lipped. The piece is a fine example of elaborate high-style.

Figure 89 shows a Norwich-area version of the block-and-shell chest-on-chest form. Dwarf cabriole legs, with distinctive claw-and-ball feet, support the lower case, which is broad in mass and made to look large in scale by the use of three instead of four drawers. The skirt is scrolled in S-shapes that seem to reflect the wave motif found on many English pieces of the 1740's; the shell carving of the drawer is well conceived and as carefully carved as Newport examples. The upper case introduces a basic change from figure 88, however: the side pilasters, with acanthus-carved capitals, reflect the Massachusetts idea of pilaster strips (found also on other Connecticut pieces) instead of engaged fluted quarter-columns. In addition, instead of leaving the upper case plain, the blocking has been carried up, and the center top drawer carved to a New England fan. The pediment, which lacks the sweeping curve of the Newport example, is flattened and the movement pushed toward the center; the finials have a fine reel and ring turning below acanthus-carved urns that hold loosely moving corkscrew flames. Made

89

90

91

90. Highboy (high-style), Rhode Island, Newport, 1755–1790. *Yale University Art Gallery; The Mabel Brady Garvan Collection.*

91. Highboy (country), eastern Connecticut,
1755–1810. *Yale University Art Gallery;
The Mabel Brady Garvan Collection.*

92. Highboy (country), eastern Connecticut,
1755–1810. *Dr. James P. Morrill.*

92

in cherry, the whole attitude of the piece is provincial in comparison with a Newport example, but when studied carefully, it begins to make sense. On the whole, the piece shows great imagination and attention to detail; it has majesty, humor, and a delight in patterned surfaces, and is typical of one extreme of Connecticut work.

The Newport highboy in figure 90 shows the same flat front façade and squared mass as the related chest-on-chest in figure 86. The front utilizes a flat shell placed within the skirt—rather than on it as in Philadelphia, or within a drawer as in Massachusetts—enabling the skin of the front façade to remain unbroken. The straight front is supported on squared cabriole legs, continuing the straightness down to the sinewy ankles and the exquisitely carved open-talon claw-and-ball front feet. The flatness of the drawers is carried up by the paired applied plaques above, and the central board of the closed bonnet intensifies the feeling that the design is being forced into, or held within, a two-plane surface. To focus the interest at the front plane, the rear feet have been shaped to simple club forms. This does not imply that the piece is transitional (that is, between Queen Anne and Chippendale); rather, it is a means, used on many Rhode Island pieces in the second half of the eighteenth century, of maintaining the design as a frontal one.

This highboy, incidentally, provides another example of deliberate artifice in the construction of the legs. As on many Rhode Island highboys, the legs are detachable; the lower case is made with the sides joined directly to the front, and the legs extend up inside to be glued into the corners. To make it look like a piece with the front skirt actually tenoned into the top of the front leg, the outer edges of the front skirt have been veneered with vertical grain as if they were an extension of the leg.

The Connecticut highboy in figure 91 utilizes much of the same Rhode Island tradition. Squared cabriole legs are glued within the skirt, rather than acting as corner posts; the shell is placed within the skirt, although it employs one of the Connecticut designs of undulating lobes. Above, the proportions are not unlike Rhode Island's, but the columns are free-standing and rope-turned (a form virtually unknown outside Connecticut ex-

cept on a few pieces from the Connecticut Valley of Massachusetts, and from New Jersey). The upper case is divided from the pediment as in figure 84 by a straight cornice. The rosettes are painted red, and the central pine cone black, as in Connecticut doorways. The three visible woods were not intended to be disguised by paint: the legs are maple, the case uses cherry, and the twisted rope-turned columns butternut.

In the high-style piece all parts are integrated, blended together to form one unit; in the country piece, separate units are placed in conjunction: legs, shell, columns, rosettes, and pine cone.

The highboy in figure 92—another Connecticut interpretation, perhaps by the same man as figure 91—again utilizes a Rhode Island undulating skirt of reverse curves interrupted by small breaks. The detachable legs, feet, rope-turning, and shell in the central top drawer are similar in shape to those on figure 91, and it has the naïve openness of a fine country piece.

The Newport high-style chest of drawers, figure 93, uses three deep drawers to provide a spacious sense of design but not the openness of the base of the Connecticut chest-on-chest (figure 89). Typical of the best work of Newport is the small overhang of the top, which is supported by a simple, beautifully shaped cove molding that physically and visually joins it to the case of drawers below. The upper drawer is decorated with three shells, two positive and one negative, so exquisitely carved that this treatment has been called "cameo-like." These shells cap the vertical three-part division of the front facade, which holds in tension the horizontal movement of the drawers. Below the lower drawer, a molding moves outward over the bold reverse-curve bracket feet with blocked and scrolled edging. The brasses are bold and act as major design elements, marking the six rectangles that enrich the two lower drawers and elaborating the area between the recessed and projecting shells.

The country cherry chest of drawers, figure 94, is another New London County variation on a Newport design. Similarly, the top is supported and connected to the case by a broad cove-shaped molding above the shell drawer, less subtle in shape than the Newport one, and the front is enriched by blocking and shells. The bottom of the

93

93. Chest of drawers (high-style), Rhode Island, Newport, 1755–1795. *Courtesy, Henry Francis du Pont Winterthur Museum.*

94. Chest of drawers (country), Connecticut, New London County, 1755–1810. *Courtesy, Henry Francis du Pont Winterthur Museum.*

94

95

96

case is enclosed by a molding, which moves out over abbreviated cabriole legs with long horizontally scrolled and pierced knee brackets and claw and ball feet; the rear legs are high reverse-curve bracket feet. This country cherry example lacks the boldness of scale and the powerful units found in the Newport piece: the shells do not project as grandly; the brasses are reduced in scale (perhaps because it is a later piece); and the cabriole front legs force the mass into the air, losing the chunky, tight-knit quality of the Newport piece. But instead, we have a new and delightful experience. Different motifs, such as a scrolled knee bracket, add an enrichment of decoration. Gone are the simple legs that made the shells so prominent on the Newport example. In fact, the love of pattern and eye entertainment has taken precedence over simple, bold, direct elegance. Both are great pieces, but the greatness is of a different kind.

The chests of drawers, figures 95 to 97, are of the style that followed the blocked chests of drawers—the Early Classical Revival period of 1790 to 1815. The elaborate, elegant chest of drawers in

figure 95 has a format that is usually associated with Portsmouth, New Hampshire, but its ultra-sophistication suggests that it is perhaps from Boston. Four ungraduated drawers are poised upon long, French, bracket feet, which move up to a skirt shaped to paired arches either side of a central plaque. A sense of lift is usually given to chests of drawers by graduating the drawers, placing the deeper ones at the base; here lift is given by the movement of the bracket feet and the central plaque. The facade is serpentined, with the movement beginning at the corner of the case rather than at a chamfered edge or an inch or two in from the outer edge; the case around the drawers and the edge of the top are both decorated with cross-banded veneer; patterned, line inlay appears in the skirt and on the edge of the top. The entire piece is restrained and refined in detailing, and the façade is raised to the highest degree of elegance by the feather-grained veneer. This pattern is arranged so that the broad part of the feather is placed to the right on the top drawer, to the left on the second drawer, to the right on the third

95. Chest of drawers (high-style), probably eastern Massachusetts, Boston area, 1790–1815. *Yale University Art Gallery; The Mabel Brady Garvan Collection.*

96. Chest of drawers (country), possibly New Hampshire, 1790–1815. *Yale University Art Gallery; The Mabel Brady Garvan Collection.*

97. Chest of drawers (primitive), Connecticut, possibly Kent area, signed Bates How, dated 1795. *Yale University Art Gallery; The Mabel Brady Garvan Collection.*

97

drawer, and to the left on the fourth drawer. The alternation introduces a perfect balance which would not have been achieved had the bases of the feathers been placed all one way. This piece cries out for the most elegant way of life, the most formal milieu.

Figure 96, a country piece, is of the same date as the preceding chest, but the sophisticated serpentine line is lacking. The legs, although high in form, do not have the outward kick, and the skirt is less elegant in its definition. Yet this piece was made by a man who understood his wood and devised a form that would make the most of its elaborate native graining. He used a simple swelling shape so taut in its surface that it looks almost helium-filled, a thin skin overfilled with pressure from inside. The simple bowing presents the incredible grain in the best possible way: on graduated drawers, it moves up first to the left, then to the right, and at last to the left again. Here too there is sophistication, but of a different kind to the suavity of the high-style example.

Figure 97 is a primitive example from Connect-

icut; as is typical of primitives, it combines forms from an early and a later date. Early are the broad overhang of the top, the rope-turned engaged quarter-columns and skirt, and the claw-and-ball feet. Later in date is the use of a reverse-serpentine or oxbow front, which introduces a smooth rolling surface that is related to the movement of the more sophisticated serpentine form but seems also in part to be a carryover of the earlier idea of blocking. The brasses are the kind normally associated with the period 1780 to 1810 and, as with so many Connecticut pieces, the basic wood is cherry. This piece, which has considerable charm, achieves a smooth, rather flat façade bound and contained by the projecting top and the rope-turning at the sides and base. The whole is supported on small claw-and-ball feet that here have been reduced almost to the mass of French bracket feet, a size in keeping with the more classical nature of the reverse-serpentine front. With this combination of features it is not surprising that the piece was in fact recently discovered to be dated late in the eighteenth century. It is inscribed:

98

98. Dressing table (high-style), eastern Massachusetts, 1740–1760. *Courtesy of Israel Sack, Inc., N.Y.C.*

99. Dressing table (high-style), Boston, Massachusetts, 1740–1760. *Courtesy, Henry Francis du Pont Winterthur Museum.*

100. Dressing table (primitive), New England or New Jersey, 1730–1750. *Courtesy of Israel Sack, Inc., N.Y.C.*

"This buro was made/in the year of our Lord/ 1795 by/Bates How"—a period when these later features could be known in rural Connecticut.

Figure 98 shows one of the purest, most direct statements of the Queen Anne form of dressing table. Although it lacks the more elaborate decoration of shells or carving often accompanying such high-quality pieces, it has instead the direct pureness of the plain high-style design carried out in the very finest manner, something always possible but seldom achieved. A rectangular top with re-entrant front corners crowns a case holding one long over three short drawers, the central one wider, and all are enriched with nicely shaped polished brasses. The skirt, responding to the three lower drawers, is shaped to three simple horizontal rectangular cutouts, with C-shaped ends; this C-shaped movement is the same as the lips of the drawers and is repeated in the movement of the knee brackets, which swing into the outward curve of the cabriole legs and down to turned club feet. Serenely composed, this piece has the best of American qualities: it does not depend on elaborate decoration; it makes its statement simply by fine proportions and a correct tension between the parts.

The blocked dressing table in figure 99 is classified here as confused, high style. In high-style furniture, blocking is almost exclusively confined to larger case pieces which reach nearly to the floor. Cabinetmakers often did not know what to do with the skirt area, which is narrower than the drawers. When, as here, it is decorated with brasses, a slightly pinched effect is achieved. This rather naïve solution adds richness, interest, amusement, and originality, without the undue awkwardness found on many of the country pieces. The result is an interestingly patterned front on finely shaped cabriole legs.

The dressing table, figure 100, is one of the greatest of American primitives. Bold, wild, fantastic, fanciful, and exquisite, it has the power to dominate its primitive milieu. Not only does it introduce blocking, strange on a piece of this proportion, but it alters the traditional pattern and puts another positive statement in the center, using for this a broader blocking than at the sides to carry the broad concave shell below, with its wide, serpentine lower edge. The ends of the front skirt are cut to rectangles with deep C-shaped ends; the front corners of the case are masked with pilaster strips like those often found on the upper case of a chest-on-chest, particularly in Massachusetts; here, however, they not only mask the front but carry around onto the front edge of the sides. Such is the attention lavished on this piece that not only the faces of the pilasters but their narrow edges flanking the drawers are fluted. The legs are necessarily exaggerated in their movement to carry the active, bold case; and the curve at the bottom part of the cabriole, where it moves out into the ridged, somewhat pointed, multiple pad foot, is active enough to provide visual support to the mass above. The pilaster out over the knee is a feature that would be successful only on such a forceful primitive example. Dramatic and strong, this piece in the late 1960's brought one of the highest prices paid to that date for any piece of furniture.

Six examples of the small desk, figures 101 through 105, and figure 146, show variations of another useful form. The high-style desk on frame, figure 101, is a richly developed statement of a Queen Anne version. The fall lid and the drawer fronts are bordered with patterned inlay, and the skirt is shaped to four well-integrated reverse curves that move over to long, slender, elegant cabriole legs on club feet. The comparable country desk on frame, figure 146, undoubtedly by Eliphalet Chapin, has features in common with his highboy (figure 84), particularly in the shape of the skirt, the use of small brasses, and the general character of smooth, simple shapes.

The primitive desk on frame in figure 102 is possibly from Rhode Island, judging by the shape of the legs, but particularly because the mid-molding is attached to the upper case rather than the lower, and overlaps the frame. Another feature found in Rhode Island is the small square-ended pullouts for supporting the fall lid when open (as in figure 19). This desk is related to the high-style and country desks in that each skirt has four basic reverse curves, but each curve is more prominent. The two drawers make themselves more easily seen as strong horizontals than do the three drawers of the high-style piece. The legs are immediately remarkable and introduce a note of abrupt verticality, but they are carefully drawn with a

99

100

101

101. Desk on frame (high-style), eastern Massachusetts, 1730–1750. *Courtesy of Israel Sack, Inc., N.Y.C.*

102. Desk on frame (primitive), probably Rhode Island, 1740–1805. *Courtesy of Israel Sack, Inc., N.Y.C.*

103. Desk (primitive), New England, 1740–1805. *Courtesy of Israel Sack, Inc., N.Y.C.*

104. Desk on frame (primitive), New England, 1790–1820. *Courtesy of Israel Sack, Inc., N.Y.C.*

105. High desk (primitive), Maine, found in Gorham, 1750–1810. *Privately owned.*

102

103

104

105

106. Side chair (high-style), Pennsylvania, Philadelphia, 1740–1760. *Yale University Art Gallery; on loan from St. John's Episcopal Church.*

107. Side chair (high-style), Massachusetts, Boston, 1740–1760. *Yale University Art Gallery; The Mabel Brady Garvan Collection.*

108. Side chair (country), Connecticut, Wethersfield-Hartford area, 1740–1760. *Yale University Art Gallery.*

106

ring above a reel-turning, over a "straight cabriole" leg.

Another primitive slant-top desk, figure 103, continues to use Queen Anne elements although it could have been made in the nineteenth century. The legs are simply taper-turned, like the Early Classical turnings of about 1800 (instead of having the more cabriole or swelling outline of figures 102 and 109), although they terminate in club feet. The large slant top is supported, when open, on the pulled-out drawer, rather than on slides; the escutcheon on the lid is a "homemade," eight-sided piece, attached with rose-headed nails, and the drawer pull is a wooden knob. The surface is painted, and the turnings—for example, the reel-turnings at the tops of the legs—are simplified to the point where they merely break the line rather than introduce a strong design factor. In such pieces the space delineated by the legs and the bottom of the skirt is as important as the mass of the wood. Viewed from the front, the design seems to be a composite of three rectangles: the lid, the front with its rectangular drawer, and the rectan-

107

108

gular space below. Handsome and direct, the impact lies in the charm and immediacy of design.

The primitive desk on frame, figure 104, clearly states its lateness by its use of square-tapered legs, introduced into this country about 1790 and popular well into the nineteenth century; the brasses are equally late. The lower edge of the slant lid has a molding to support a book; this molding is interrupted in the middle so that the lid can be supported on a central pull support which resembles the candle slides on the front of the Joseph Brown Newport secretary (figure 20). On the side, immediately above the mid-molding, there is another slide, probably for a candle. Neat and compact in design, this piece has the same directness as the preceding desk but suffers considerably from having lost the charm of paint.

The high desk on double baluster and ring-turned legs, figure 105—recently found in Gorham, Maine—seems at first to be an early example; but the form of the feet and the slenderness of the turnings suggest the late eighteenth century, and it is probably as late as the two preceding

pieces. Similar also is the directness, forthrightness, and simplicity of the design. The top, gently slanted, uses an early form of construction with the hinges placed above. The turnings of the legs are beautifully balanced but elongated to give the desired height as well as to reflect the slender taste then in vogue; the base is connected by stretchers, using a seventeenth- and early eighteenth-century tradition; and the whole is supported on finely turned reel and bulb feet. Fortunately this piece (unlike that in figure 104) has retained its original red paint, for the presence on these primitive pieces of original paint is often one of their main assets. Here it combines with a design that can truly be called "elegant," to make one of the finest primitives.

The five Queen Anne style side chairs, figures 106 through 110, are arranged first to demonstrate the regional differences in high-style design, and then to show country and primitive interpretations. The side chair in figure 106 represents the Philadelphia Queen Anne style at its peak. The chair is a symphony of reverse curves: cabriole

109   110

legs, horseshoe-shaped seat, back posts (from the front and from the side), the additional raised curved section in the center of the crest rail, and a splat drawn—each side—to three varying curves. The whole amounts to motion, elegance, and aristocracy; it emits a sense of suave superiority. The Massachusetts chair, figure 107, is of the same period, probably from Boston. It too displays reverse curves, but the back posts break to shaped forms when viewed from the side, and the back splat is more quietly composed; in addition the chair retains, from an earlier period, turned, rather straight stretchers, which, except for the swelling of the medial and rear stretchers, do not reflect the Queen Anne movement. The final statement is of a solid, firm stance. These two chairs show the difference between the two style centers: Boston used heavier members, slower-moving curves, and a sense of weight and mass; Philadelphia drew out the parts to more elongated openness, and even the feet were pulled out to pointed pad or slipper forms. Both represent high-style, but achieved in different ways.

The Connecticut Queen Anne side chair, figure 108, belonged, along with other equally fine pieces, to one Ezekiel Porter (about 1740) in Wethersfield, Connecticut, and it is probable that it was made there or in the neighboring Hartford area. The material used was cherry, and the chair carries its original multicolored needlework seat. The design cannot be analyzed as suave and elegant like the Philadelphia example, nor, as with the Boston one, bold and forthright. Instead, it expresses one extreme of Connecticut's attitude toward design: open elegance. The legs grow out of turned club feet to rise in loose curves to a horseshoe-shaped seat, which curves in and back to the rear posts; the back posts, below the seat, are raked sharply backward at the base—a Connecticut feature; above the seat they rise to a simple, slender crest rail over a splat shaped to two reverse curves on either side, with a ring silhouette between; the splat and most of the parts are narrower than on the high-style chairs and there is a sense of space moving through the chair—as important to the design as the wood itself. It is like a

109. Side chair (primitive), New York, possibly Albany area, 1740–1805. *Yale University Art Gallery; The Mabel Brady Garvan Collection.*

110. Side chair (primitive), probably Connecticut, 1740–1805. *Privately owned.*

111. Arm chair (high-style), Rhode Island, Newport, 1740–1760. *Courtesy, Henry Francis du Pont Winterthur Museum.*

112. Arm chair (primitive), eastern Massachusetts, 1740–1805. *Mr. and Mrs. Charles L. Bybee.*

111

design pulled from taffy, stretched out, made lean and tall. In modern idiom, it resembles wire sculpture in that the open spaces are as much a part of the design as the wire. Pulled out into space, it is open and elegant in a very different way from the Philadelphia chair. Here a naïveté about form is joined with a fine sense of pattern.

The New York Queen Anne chair, figure 109, is a type made between New York and Albany. Although Queen Anne high-style designs are usually dated, with rare exceptions, as 1725 or 1730 to 1760, we know that primitive chairs like these remained popular long after that. They continued to be advertised in *The Albany Gazette*, for example, at least as late as 1803.* Appealing in a way different from the high-style or country examples, each part is boldly conceived and well executed. The splat is swelling in form, with a nice relationship to the turned front legs. And these

* Norman Rice: *New York Furniture Before 1840* (Albany, N.Y.: Albany Institute of History and Art; 1962), p. 38. The advertisement illustrated is from *The Albany Gazette* of 1799, but Mr. Rice reports similar notices as late as 1803.

112

legs, although they seem to be a carryover from the trumpet-turned ones of the William and Mary lowboys, have, in fact, the outward movement of a cabriole form. The reel-turnings at the top of the front legs are sharp and give a clear, immediate impression, and the legs terminate in turned, slanted pad feet. Only the crest rail, splat, and rail supporting the splat were cut from boards; the rest adheres to the early, easy way of creating rounded forms, by lathe, rather than employing more arduous carving. The woods are maple and tulip poplar, local woods usually painted black or red to give a rich and immediate pattern or silhouette. The related primitive (probably Connecticut) maple side chair, figure 110, has ring-turned front legs like those found on ladder backs and bannister backs, and has back posts with fine, clearly drawn turnings like those on some bannister backs. Only the crest rail and the splat introduce Queen Anne forms, but their shapes are made so as to integrate the new and old elements; the surface retains much of its original red paint, found under a nineteenth-century black, gold, and floral layer.

This sequence of Queen Anne chairs (figures 106–110) has demonstrated much about the differences in types of furniture—the variation in woods, forms and movements, final finishes, and general character. Two Queen Anne arm chairs are offered for similar comparison. The high-style Rhode Island arm chair in figure 111 shows a lean clarity that relates it to some Connecticut examples, but it has a precise starkness of line, particularly in the back, that is different. A veneered splat has been introduced, with a central panel surrounded by triple-line inlay and cross-banding, similar to English splats and related to the veneering on some of the contemporary American highboys and dressing tables. The outwardly rolled shoulders of the back posts are, in America, known only in Rhode Island. The knees show rather rudimentary carving that, although designed with a slightly heavy hand, does not greatly disturb the movement of the cabriole legs, which, with their heavy ankles, are English in nature. The shapes found in the flat stretchers are more akin to Queen Anne movement than the turned stretchers found on Massachusetts examples. Elegant and sparse, the final statement is a lean and forceful one.

113. Side chair (high-style), Pennsylvania, Philadelphia, 1755–1795. *Yale University Art Gallery; The Mabel Brady Garvan Collection.*

114. Side chair (country), Connecticut, East Windsor, 1771–1807. *Yale University Art Gallery; The Mabel Brady Garvan Collection.*

115. Side chair (primitive), New England, possibly central Connecticut Valley, 1755–1810. *Yale University Art Gallery; The Mabel Brady Garvan Collection.*

116. Side chair (primitive), New Hampshire, 1768–1810. *The Metropolitan Museum of Art; gift of Mrs. J. Linsley Blair.*

113

114

115

116

117

118

The primitive Massachusetts Queen Anne arm chair in figure 112 has an almost identical lean, elegant stance, but the elements, except for the back and feet, are a continuation of William and Mary forms. There is a superb attention to detail, as in the chamfering of the squared areas of the front legs and the edges of the arms. The turnings of the front stretcher are, although not massive or particularly bold, nicely balanced and clean in line; the paint that enriches the surface is perhaps of a later date, although elements of the chair suggest that it was made rather late in the eighteenth century.

The Chippendale side chairs in figures 113 to 116 present a sequence of interpretations similar to that illustrated by the Queen Anne group. The upper part of the back of figure 113 was shown in figure 46. This chair is one of the finest Philadelphia expressions and dramatically projects the attitude to design that underlies the achievement of Philadelphia high-style furniture: balance of repeated design units or motifs, at its best. Starting at beautifully carved claw-and-ball feet, the legs surge upward to acanthus-carved knees; the acanthus carving springs from the scroll of the knee

bracket, scrolling up toward the seat rail. From under the leaves outlining the bracket, more leafage flows out and down the leg toward the center tendon of the foot. The center of the knee is carved to a partial flower; the movement of the knee bracket continues into the seat rail, which is horizontally shaped to lighten it as it moves toward the central, applied, convex shell; the shell rays downward and is carved to positive and negative lobes; this is repeated in a larger form on the crest rail, but is there reversed to ray up and out. The ears of the crest rail are carved to boldly knuckled forms with a raised center flanked by side scrolls; the bowed line of the crest rail flows down from the ears, behind the central shell, into the splat where the outer straps terminate in scrolls. Below, three ribs rise from the shoe to divide, join, and terminate in scrolls below the upper scrolls; the upper and lower strapwork is joined by overlapping central ribs; and the positive and negative carving of the shell is repeated in the fluting of the back posts. The chair is carefully balanced, each unit exquisitely manufactured, every feature responding to and blending with the rest; the final statement is a sophisticated, integrated whole.

119

117. Upholstered arm chair (high-style), eastern Massachusetts, 1775–1795. *Yale University Art Gallery; The Mabel Brady Garvan Collection.*

118. Upholstered arm chair (primitive), New England, 1760–1810. *Mr. and Mrs. Bayard Ewing.*

119. Upholstered arm chair (rustic), American, 1800–1850. *Old Sturbridge Village photograph.*

120. Side chair (rustic), New England, nineteenth century. *Privately owned.*

121. Arm chair (rustic), New England, nineteenth century. *Courtesy of Shelburne Museum.*

120

121

122

122. Side chair (high-style), probably Rhode Island, possibly Newport, 1790–1815. *Courtesy of Israel Sack, Inc., N.Y.C.*

123. Commode chair (country), probably Connecticut, possibly New London County, 1790–1815. *Courtesy, Museum of Fine Arts, Boston.*

124. Arm chair (primitive), New England, probably Rhode Island, 1790–1815. *The Metropolitan Museum of Art; gift of Mrs. Russell Sage.*

The Chapin chair, figure 114, was made for a different context. Having worked in Philadelphia, Chapin continued to use some Philadelphia ideas: the rounded back posts below the seat, through tenons (the tenons of the joints between the side rails and the back posts pass completely through the back post and are exposed behind), and Philadelphia-type corner blocks. Here, however, similarity to Philadelphia ceases. The front feet are more knuckled and deeply carved, the cabriole legs more forceful in movement, and the front seat rail undecorated. The ears do not have a raised center; they are more like the Massachusetts ear in figure 45, straighter across the ends, and they have a central crease very popular in New York. The central shell of the crest rail is unlike the Philadelphia shell, lacking the flutes between the positive lobes; it resembles rather the New York shell found on the famous Livingston chairs, or the typical New York gadrooning (figure 21). The strapwork is composed of four C-shapes that come from the crest rail (as on Rhode Island, New York, and some Massachusetts chairs), and the upper half is separated from the lower strapwork by a carved line (as in Massachusetts). Chapin produced a chair that is powerful and strong, not at all in the Philadelphia taste. Indeed, the three Philadelphia elements, back legs, through tenons, and corner blocks, are the least visible parts of the chair. Instead of being elegant, it is powerful and forceful. The action begins at the base of the back posts, which are placed close together to spring strongly outward toward the ears; there, the movement is caught and brought back through the crest rail to the splat, where it actively scrolls in upon itself to terminate in exquisite scroll terminals. The design is one of action, movement, and tense scrolling rather than suave refinement. Chapin,

123

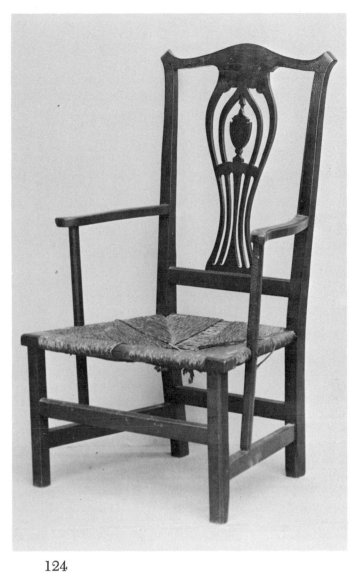

124

like a few other Connecticut cabinetmakers, achieved expressions in cherry that are today best known in plastics. He produced smooth, almost soft curves, seen in the way the front face of the crest rail rolls backward on either side of the shell; in Philadelphia this area is kept flat and vertical. The ears, too, seem almost plastic in quality as if they were cast from a smooth, hard material. This surface can be obtained in very few woods; close-grained cherry, which carves like hard soap, is one of them.

The side chair, figure 115, is part of the third design tradition: it shows that composite of styles so typical of primitive work. The crest rail and splat are in the Chippendale mode; the ideas for the rest of the chair are drawn from at least thirty years, and two style periods, earlier. The base of the splat rests upon a rail above the seat, rather than penetrating into it, to allow for the rush seat,

which must wrap around the rear rail and not be interrupted by a splat (a few rush-seated chairs do have a slit in the rail, in front of the shoe of the splat, but a rail like the one used here is far more common). The legs are block and baluster-turned, and terminate in Spanish feet; the stretchers are baluster-turned. The wood is maple and originally carried a coat of red paint. As is traditional in these primitive designs, the back—the immediately visible part—is the most updated area; the base continues an earlier, more easily made design.

Another primitive chair, figure 116, was made by a member of the Dunlap family, and here (as in figures 43 and 44) are introduced notes of originality typical of provincial folk work. As in the Philadelphia chair (figure 113), there is a repetition between the upper and lower sections: the molding of the front legs finds a response in the molding of the front of the back posts above

125

126

the seat that continues onto the ears; the molding on the stretchers is repeated on the rail above the seat, and the shell is repeated. But in spite of this response between the upper and lower sections, the final expression is very different from the Philadelphia example. Bold, strong, straight verticals thrust upward to superb, large ears; these vertical posts are connected by strong horizontal members: the crest rail (which has the same shape as the top of the ear), the rail supporting the bottom of the splat, and the front seat rail, placed not, as on high-style pieces, between the side rails but between the front legs. The piece is constructed like a seventeenth-century chest, with strong corner posts and connecting rails, and has the immediate appeal of strong, direct pattern.

Upholstered furniture also fits into the basic groupings. Figures 117 to 119 are typical of high-style, primitive, and rustic types. All three are equally functional but they breathe different personalities. The eastern Massachusetts chair (figure 117) shows a sophisticated integration of

vertical and horizontal wooden and upholstered elements and a fine repetition of molded surfaces. The lines are clean and distinct and the whole uses the best kind of precise detail. The primitive chair (figure 118) also uses squared legs and stretchers, backward-curving arm supports, and a bowed crest rail. It has, however, a rugged intimacy not present in the high-style chair; for example, it has a front rather than a medial stretcher. Figure 119 shows one of the few rustic pieces preserved; undoubtedly, such pieces were discarded as soon as "finer" ones could be obtained. To make this chair, the upper half of an ordinary barrel was shaped to an arched back and arms; a seat was installed and the whole well padded and upholstered. The wonderfully patterned material and the nice shaping of the arms and back turn a functional piece into a fascinating personal object. This characteristic of rustic pieces can be seen even more clearly on two remarkable unupholstered examples. The rustic chair in figure 120 (like figure 119) is a "homemade" piece which in

125. Card table (high-style), eastern Massachusetts, probably Boston, 1790–1815. *Yale University Art Gallery; The Mabel Brady Garvan Collection.*

126. Card table (country), northern New England, 1790–1815. *Courtesy of Israel Sack, Inc., N.Y.C.*

127. Card table (primitive), northern New England, 1790–1830. *Privately owned.*

127

this case is a pine log that is hollow throughout; the front of the log was cut away above, and a seat of three boards nailed in place. The rustic arm chair in figure 121 is a partial log turned on its side; it has a raised back, and the center part of the lower edge is cut away to leave "arms." The whole is supported on four sticks. Both pieces have distinction and personality.

A group of later chairs that clearly show the difference between high-style, country, and primitive is given in figures 122 to 124. The chair in figure 122 is precisely defined to a clear, formal statement of the developed taste of about 1800. This chair goes a step further than most of the same design (which are found in many areas of Rhode Island and in the Hartford area of Connecticut), for it introduces triple-line inlay on the front legs, back posts, and crest rail. This extra refinement, the high quality of the carving, the shape of the basic units, and the bowing of the front seat rail all render the piece one of the most developed and sophisticated expressions of this not-uncommon form. The country commode chair, figure 123, utilizes the same basic design while introducing other motifs, perhaps in a way that is unique. These motifs are not original creations; it is the way they are used that is surprising. The central shells of the crest rail and the base of the splat are demi-patera forms found on the base of some related chair splats; the "stuck-on" ears are known on other examples but do not belong on shield-shaped forms; and the deep skirt displays a carved shell large enough for a desk or chest of drawers. The form of the shell has caused this chair to be assigned to the Norwich–New London area of Connecticut, although "stuck-on" ears are known in the New Jersey–Maryland area as well. The concept has country naïveté in the way it brings together motifs and detailing and uses ideas from both the Chippendale and the Early Classical Revival periods. It scatters them about in a way that is far from high-style, but fortunately the creator's eye was sufficiently good for the combination, although not of a traditional nature, to make an interesting resolution. To us, at this distance in time, it has the amusement of whimsy or personal caprice.

The primitive chair, figure 124, employs the same splat as the two preceding examples, but introduces it into a chair that would otherwise be classified as a Chippendale form; the squared legs are not tapered and the crest rail is a simple bow with ears; the housing of the splat in a rail above the seat is necessary because of the rush seat. This is not the work of a man who tried to make a form like that in figure 122 and failed; no crude attempts at inlay have been made, and the front legs are not tapered. Instead, it is a chair that must have said to its maker and buyer, "I am within the new style as far as taste demands, but I am made by the means available and for my personal setting." It was not only a question of economics or the maker's training but of the chair's complete suitability to its context. It is impossible to know whether the original owner would rather have had a chair like the one in figure 122, but in all probability the question did not arise. The high-style chair belonged to a different world from that in which the owner of the primitive chair moved.

The three card tables, figures 125 to 127, also show different attitudes. That in figure 125 has almost a surplus of elegant elements. The skirt, with its bowed front and reverse-curve sides, its light veneer shining like satin, the top edged with flickering cross-banding and elaborate line inlay, is in turn supported by tapered legs with similar veneer, which terminate in finely tapered feet below inlayed cuffs. The whole design is obviously cosmopolitan. The country tiger-maple table, figure 126, utilizes solid woods to achieve its shimmering surface. As in the preceding table, the front is bowed and the sides reverse-curved, but the legs and feet are not as sharply tapered. The piece is heavier in appearance, and the wood itself is given the major role in presenting a bold, forceful, and solidified design.

The third card table, figure 127, is even stockier. The rectangular top is pine with cleated ends, and the legs taper to the floor without more sharply tapering feet; its utility is increased by the drawer in the front skirt. There is, however, an attempt at elaboration: although the entire piece is painted red, the drawer front is made of tiger

maple and shows through the paint to make it appear as though the whole piece is of patterned wood. (This not-uncommon New England practice was found also on the Salem highboy, figure 76.)

The first stands shown in figures 128–136 are from an earlier period than the preceding tables. The first elaborate high-style piece with piecrust top (figure 128) is a richly developed interpretation of a form that is almost never found outside high-style design. But, although it is rich, it does not use as much elaboration as comparable highly developed English pieces. The components are easily read; each part has its distinct form and character. The carved decoration enhances rather than erodes the basic elements. This stand is assigned to Philadelphia because of the carving and because piecrust shaping seldom occurs in America except on tea tables or stands made in that city. The stand in figure 129 is equally sophisticated in line. A perfect reverse-curve tripod base supports the column, which has exquisitely drawn and well-balanced turnings below a simple but beautifully edged oval top. The piece illustrates New England plain high-style and is branded on the base of the pedestal "W. King" of Salem(?), Massachusetts.

The country stand in figure 130 illustrates a different taste. In no way can it be considered suave or elegant, sophisticated in line, or ideally balanced. The legs are too slender for the column; the column above the urn form thickens at its center; the inlaid top crowns a heavy substructure that holds a small drawer. Yet it shows a delight in form, and a good balance of interesting, although not exquisite, shapes.

Figure 131 is obviously a primitive stand. Large legs, with massive feet, are cut from boards and tenoned into the shaft above a baluster and bell-form drop; the turning, above the legs, is a large baluster form; the top is simple, without decoration, and is made of two boards held by a large cleat. Later white paint has been removed so that most of the original red-orange paint is now visible. It seems clear that the right rear foot never had the shaping found on the top of the other two, for the original paint also covers its upper surface. This rather crude but amusing table was made by someone who created bold interpretations of mo-

128

129

128. Stand (high-style), Pennsylvania, Philadelphia, 1755–1795. *Courtesy of Israel Sack, Inc., N.Y.C.*

129. Stand (high-style), eastern Massachusetts, possibly Salem, stamped "W. King," 1780–1800. *Courtesy of Israel Sack, Inc., N.Y.C.*

130

131

133

134

132

130. Stand (country), New England, 1790–1815. *Courtesy of Israel Sack, Inc., N.Y.C.*
131. Stand (primitive), northern New England, 1810–1840. *Courtesy of Roger Bacon.*
132. Stand (primitive), northern New England, 1790–1830. *Mr. and Mrs. Bayard Ewing.*
133. Stand (primitive), probably Pennsylvania, 1820–1850. *Courtesy of The Henry Ford Museum, Dearborn, Michigan.*
134. Stand (primitive), northern New England, 1750–1810. *Courtesy, Richard W. Withington, Inc., Oliver E. Williams auction, 1966.*
135. Stand (primitive), probably New England, 1750–1810. *Courtesy of Israel Sack, Inc., N.Y.C.*
136. Stand or Stool (rustic), America or Canada, probably nineteenth century. *Courtesy of Shelburne Museum.*

135

136

137

tifs borrowed from more elaborate designs. Since the maker had a lathe and other equipment available, he could have produced something more nearly like the preceding stand, but he was not attempting to do so. He was thinking along different lines, working within other demands and attitudes toward what was acceptable and right in his setting.

The wonderful green primitive stand (figure 132) is made simply but with strict attention to sound construction methods. The three stick legs are housed into the large base of the shaft and secured by pins that penetrate into the legs through the base; the large ball base is a separate unit from the shaft above, with the shaft housed into it and secured with pins; and the shaft is connected to a circular "cleat" under the top. Despite the fine construction, it is hard to find elements in this stand that could be considered classic in outline. Instead, it is a composite of bulges and simple turnings that recall baluster forms, the whole perched on three sticks; yet a fascinating, pleasing design was created. Particularly impor-

tant is the fact that this piece has never been refinished, for had it lost its early paints, now worn to a marvelous rich somber green, much of its personality would have been stripped away.

The stand in figure 133 was perhaps made by a man who had no lathe available; or, more likely, since the feet and knobs appear turned, he chose to make his object without the help of one. The function of the piece has been maintained; indeed, it has been enhanced with drawers that could serve for sewing materials or other necessities. Here is the humor that often comes with originality, the enjoyment of a personal way of solving a problem. The balance of the parts, although unusual, is such that they reinforce each other so that the final

137. Dressing table (high-style), Pennsylvania, Philadelphia, 1755–1795. *Museum of Art, Rhode Island School of Design.*

138. Dressing table (high-style country), Pennsylvania, Lancaster County, 1775–1810. *The Metropolitan Museum of Art.*

138

expression is not awkward. Everything about the piece is of a similar expression or taste. No single feature says that it does not belong. Had a very elaborate high-style element been introduced, the design might have fallen apart and the whole become hideous. In the same way, the T-base stand (figure 134) is a primitive object of great charm with a wide interplay of unusual forms.

The immediate contrast between the pieces in figures 135 and 136 illustrates the gulf between primitive and rustic. The adjustable candle stand (figure 135) is, like the preceding piece, achieved without the benefit of elaborate shaping. It is constructed, instead, of simple sticks put together in a well-balanced way to achieve a useful, serviceable object. Although primitive in expression, it shows a genuine synthesis in which a man has imposed his character on the materials; the balance of horizontals and verticals atop the crossed arch base is well conceived, and the piece has in addition movable parts, always intriguing to the beholder. The rustic stand (figure 136), on the other hand, was made from a trunk or branch with four conven-

iently arranged branches that now form the legs. It is not a constructed piece, merely a clever selection from nature.

In order to illustrate the main subgroups as clearly as possible, controversial objects—those that for one reason or another do not fit easily into a single category—have not so far been included. The dressing tables in figures 137 and 138, however, illustrate this problem. Figure 137 is a fine high-style Philadelphia Chippendale dressing table; in every way its detailing is first-rate and it fits easily into its group. That in figure 138 does not fit easily into any group. It is well proportioned in the high-style tradition; indeed, it was once catalogued as the work of William Savery of Philadelphia, although it is now believed to be from rural Pennsylvania, perhaps Lancaster. It is in the handling of the carving that a country or even a primitive element of some magnitude is introduced. The work is very different from that on the great Philadelphia highboy (figure 17); the carving is coarser, more rugged and congested, and instead of being graceful it is tightly patterned.

Other such examples of mixed character do exist, particularly when two skills were needed. Here the maker was very close to the high-style tradition, but the carver turned the piece into a country statement.

The separation of seventeenth-century items into four categories also presents particular problems, for the division into attitudes is less obvious. It should be emphasized that at this early date there were, quite simply, very few cabinetmakers. Often a categorization is based on a regional difference rather than a difference in type. The eastern-Massachusetts press cupboard in figure 139 is one of the richest American expressions of the form. Not only does it utilize exquisitely turned and well-balanced decoration, but the decoration is applied to well-defined, geometrical patterns. This is a rich new statement of a Renaissance expression that came to America by way of England. The Connecticut press cupboard in figure 27 has as beautifully drawn detail, but it is removed from the most elaborate Renaissance tradition by the introduction of the large carved areas in the bottom section. It should, perhaps, be classified as "country," and does in fact come from central Connecticut, while that in figure 139 is from an urban area. The press cupboard from New Hampshire in figure 77, on the other hand, is in the peasant or primitive tradition. This design originated in the northwest of England, where the elaborately paneled form was reduced to board construction. Its importance lies in its charm, its smallness, its amusing decoration, and its balance of rectangular shapes, and it is best understood as primitive.

Because such controversial pieces as these do exist, it should be stressed again that the terms employed here have been used simply to make it easier to perceive the nature of individual pieces. Every object ultimately makes its own statement, and any device used to reveal this more fully remains only a device.

139. Press cupboard, eastern Massachusetts, 1670–1710. *Courtesy of Israel Sack, Inc., N.Y.C.*

139

CHAPTER VII

Evaluating
&
Collecting

140

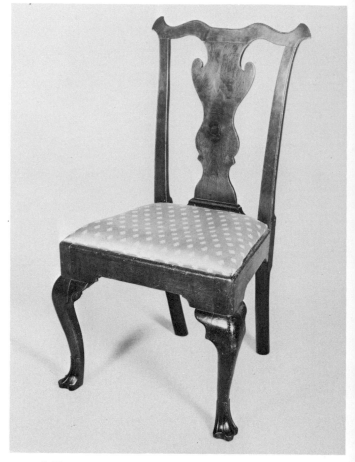

141

142

143

140. Side chair, Pennsylvania, Philadelphia, 1745–1795. *Yale University Art Gallery; The Mabel Brady Garvan Collection.*

141. Side chair, Pennsylvania, Philadelphia, 1745–1795. *Yale University Art Gallery; The Mabel Brady Garvan Collection.*

142. Windsor arm chair, American, probably New York or New England, 1750–1810. *Yale University Art Gallery; gift of C. Sanford Bull.*

143. Windsor arm chair, Connecticut, Lisbon, branded "Ebenezer Tracy," 1764–1803. *Yale University Art Gallery; The Mabel Brady Garvan Collection.*

The great early collectors and students of American furniture—men like Irving W. Lyon, Luke Vincent Lockwood, and Wallace Nutting—sought examples of American furniture in what to us seems an indiscriminate manner. The late nineteenth and early twentieth century was an era when everything made in America was a new and wonderful discovery. A seventeenth-century Carver chair found in a farmhouse, or on the porch, was a new revelation, a statement about early times. Today the situation is different, for so much American furniture is known that discriminating students and buyers have trained their eyes and are objective about their acquisitions.

An important aspect of such training is the understanding of the features that make an object of quality stand out within its type, whether it be high-style, country, primitive, or rustic. To pretend that an object is great when it is only second-rate means the beginning of endless frustration, and is a poor substitute for the pleasure of owning great pieces. It becomes tedious always to have to excuse the presence of an object by saying, "That was an early purchase," or, "I know that's not one of the best, but I like it." Because so many kinds of collections are possible, and because so many types of American furniture exist, anyone seeking to form a collection, whether small or large, should spend enough time with books and objects to have a clear idea of the sort of furniture he is looking for and why. If a buyer decides to form a high-style collection, he will need considerable sums of money; less is required for country, and even less for primitive.

It is far easier to buy than it is to sell objects purchased inadvertently. For this reason, before venturing into buying, a would-be collector is well advised to associate himself with someone who has the training and knowledge to guide him. The

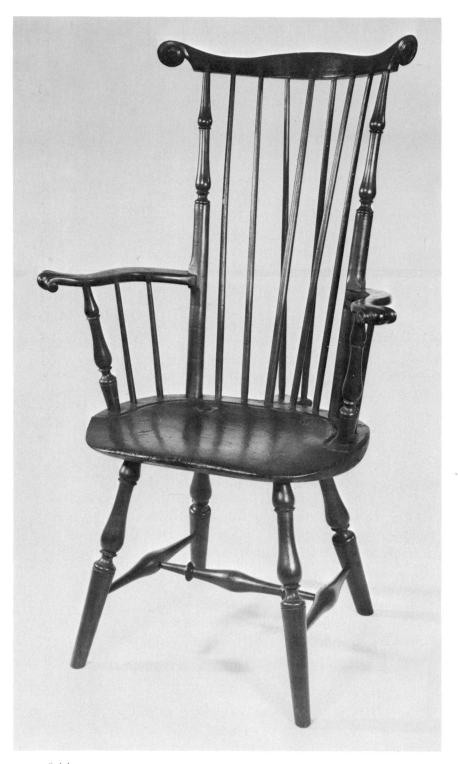

144

prices of American forms have reached the level where it is quite ridiculous for an untrained person to venture into an extremely complex field; in addition, fakes are an endless trap for the unwary.

Apart from clear intentions, a sophisticated buyer should be schooled in two areas. First, his eyes should be so trained that he immediately responds to quality; and secondly, he needs to understand the way in which genuine pieces were made, and how fakers work. Once a collector's purpose is defined, he will be more able to avoid buying an object because it is *almost* what he wants. If he wants a high-style collection, he will not settle for a country example of a form; if it is to be a country collection, he will not be seduced by a high-style form that has become battered by time and therefore seems to have taken on a rural flavor. And with proper thought and training he will not buy bad high-style and call it country. A clear purpose is the first priority, even if a mixed collection—perhaps the most interesting as well as the most difficult of all buying—is desired.

Some of the problems that confront a buyer as soon as he tries to make choices are illustrated by the two solid splat chairs in figures 140 and 141. Both are Philadelphia examples made between 1750 and 1795. This form has been called "transitional" in style, because these chairs have the solid splat and trifid feet of the Queen Anne style and the bowed crest rail of the Chippendale period; evidence proves, however, that they were made throughout the second half of the eighteenth century. The first difference to be noted between them is one of quality. On the chair in figure 140 the form of the trifid feet, carved to three projecting parts, is recalled in the carving of the shells of the knees; this shell form is again repeated on the skirt and recalled in the asymmetrical shell on the crest rail; the cabriole form of the leg moves the eye from the foot up to the knee, with its scrolled knee brackets, then to the shell area of the front seat rail; the back posts bow backward to bold,

144. Windsor arm chair, possibly New England, 1750–1810. *Yale University Art Gallery; The Mabel Brady Garvan Collection.*

145. Windsor arm chair, possibly New England, 1750–1810. *Yale University Art Gallery; The Mabel Brady Garvan Collection.*

scrolled ears that recall the scrolls of the knee brackets. The edge-molded crest rail curves gracefully toward the splat, which is composed of multiple reverse curves. Beginning under the crest rail, reverse curves swing out to the large, scrolled ears of the splat; the bold movement of the ears is part of the reverse curve to the waist, from which it reverse-curves to a fret and then in a fourth curve to the shoe. The back is bowed forward, presenting this superb splat like the chest of a pouter pigeon. Each area of the chair has bold, sophisticated movement; each reverse-curve line is strong and forceful. In contrast, figure 141 shows a lack of sophistication that places it outside of the most desirable forms of American furniture. Stubby feet support stiff front legs, the bowing of the back is minimal, and the ears move into a crest rail with a flat central area.

If the original owner did not want to pay for a central decoration, a shell or one of many other possibilities, the cabinetmaker should have introduced a more interesting line of movement than a straight center; a straight line in the midst of curves nearly always deadens a design. With the same amount of labor the center could have curved down or up, responding to the curves on either side. Under the crest rail the splat moves down in C-shapes to ears that are so ill-defined they barely scroll, but seem mere projections. The reverse-curve line moves from them to a waist that looks pinched or corseted rather than graceful, and the use of a board with an off-centered knot further reduces the quality. Some might be tempted to call this a country example, but it seems instead a bad high-style piece.

The second problem illustrated by these chairs is the fact that the aesthetically inferior of the two might well cost a purchaser as much or more than the other: it belonged to George Washington and its mate is at Mount Vernon. The setting of monetary value on a piece because of historic associations has introduced major problems into collecting. It is possible to define a collection as one of memorabilia, which is particularly relevant for historic houses or for people with a deep interest in a certain historic figure. But paying more simply because Washington sat in a chair has nothing to do with furniture as art. It has a value, but not one that relates to quality.

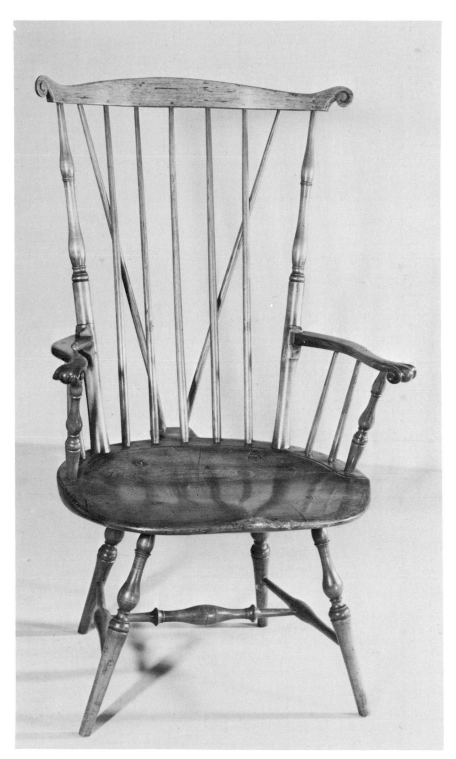

145

Another instance, perhaps subtler, of the tension between art and documentation is provided by the bow-back, continuous-arm Windsors in figures 142 and 143, which have many features in common. The first has one of the most elegant lifts to its back rail to be found in this great type of American furniture. The arm moves into the back, which sweeps over the spindles; the spindles are rayed in a sophisticated spread like the fan of a peacock tail; the seat is handsomely shaped, and the front legs are boldly turned to thick and thin areas in order to define beautiful baluster forms; these leg turnings are recalled again under the front of the arms. The whole chair is a perfect balance of thrust and counterthrust. The chair in figure 143 has fine turnings and a well-shaped seat, with a brace to support the back—considered a desirable feature as its spokes often make an interesting counterthrust to those of the back. But here they only intensify the gap that has been left for them in the center; it looks as though a tooth is missing. The maker should have used an odd number of back spokes, placing one in the center. If both these chairs were placed on the market, the one with the "missing tooth" would be preferred by some: it is branded by its maker, Ebenezer Tracy, of Lisbon, Connecticut, which does, indeed, make it useful as historical evidence.

The brace-back Windsors, figures 144 and 145, have almost every detail in common: scrolled ears terminate the crest rail of the braced back, with side posts turned to superimposed baluster forms, above reverse-curved, knuckled arms, in turn above a shaped seat holding baluster-turned legs and swell-turned stretchers. Although similar in detailing, the final statements of the two chairs are extraordinarily different. In figure 144 the thrust is all vertical; even the spokes of the braces are more vertically oriented. Everything is tighter in design. Taking just the baluster turnings of the back posts below the ears, in figure 144 there is a definition of turning, and a boldness of form that is not present in figure 145. In figure 145 everything is broadened: the bracing spokes diverge sharply to the right and left, further emphasizing the breadth of the back; the broader seat seems to wobble on legs which are well turned but do not relate to its scale. All in all, the visual differences are immense.

The two desks on frame, figures 146 and 147, are basically of the same date, the second half of the eighteenth century. Both are of cherry and consist of a slant top above a drawer area, with the upper section contained within a frame with cabriole legs. The first is from Connecticut, the second from Pennsylvania. The desk in figure 146 is undoubtedly the work of Eliphalet Chapin. Its front façade is a study of five rectangular shapes horizontally oriented; the slant area provides a large mass above the smaller mass of the long thin drawer; the three rectangular drawers in the stand are focused around a central fan, and the whole is supported by the shape of the skirt. The skirt, as on Chapin's highboy (figure 84), is shaped to a central scallop, flanked on either side by paired reverse curves which move toward the reverse-curved cabriole legs; the legs terminate in well-defined shoed, club feet. The only area of movement or decoration is the fan and the shaping of the skirt and the legs. The piece in figure 147—despite its raised top molding, engaged fluted quarter-columns, and shell-carved knees—is reduced to four strong horizontals composed of the desk lid, the two drawers, and the skirt of the stand; these strong horizontals are unrelieved by an arched fan or a shaped skirt. Instead, the horizontal movement seems plunked upon stout cabriole legs. The latter are not encouraged to flow by the presence of shell-carved knees that, in defiance of convention, flare downward, nor by the ill-defined claw-and-ball feet. The Chapin desk is one of the great country examples. Its surface has the smooth, plastic quality of the great Connecticut designs, and it has an interesting play of horizontals broken by some verticals established by separating the lower drawer area into three units. The Pennsylvania version is stocky, heavy, and ill-designed. Its legs do not seem to grow out of, respond, or relate in any way to the mass they support.

In the seventeenth century, too, such differences in quality can be discussed. Figures 148 and 149 show two Connecticut press cupboards that are, undoubtedly, by the same craftsman and provide an opportunity to study quality within one man's work. Although the similarities are immediately obvious, one design reaches a much higher level than the other. In the first piece, the upper band of decoration uses corbels instead of triglyphs; the

146

146. Desk on frame, Connecticut, East Windsor, 1771–1807. *Yale University Art Gallery; The Mabel Brady Garvan Collection.*

147. Desk on frame, Pennsylvania, 1780–1810. *Yale University Art Gallery; gift of C. Sanford Bull.*

147

148

crosses of its upper doors are more horizontally oriented and are studded with five studs instead of a single diamond; it has dentils at its mid-section, enriching the division between the upper and lower case; and at either end of the drawers, the corner posts have paired split spindles rather than a single spindle. A more subtle difference is seen in the shaping of these split spindles. Those on the first piece are perhaps slightly clearer in definition—particularly the ones on the upper case, which terminate below in bolder forms rather than the stretched-out turnings found on figure 149. In short, figure 148 has stronger, more pronounced areas of decoration; the door sections are more complex and interesting; and even the two super-imposed central panels are broader and chunkier

in proportion. There is subtlety in figure 149, which uses the classical concept of moving from the simpler to the more complex: single spindles flank the drawers of the lower case and paired spindles the doors above, while the triple units of the triglyphs accent the cornice. But all this is not sufficiently interesting to make it as rich a pattern as figure 148.

148. Press cupboard, Connecticut, Durham-Madison area, 1670–1710. *Yale University Art Gallery; gift of Charles Betts.*

149. Press cupboard, Connecticut, Durham-Madison area, 1670–1710. *Yale University Art Gallery; The Mabel Brady Garvan Collection.*

149

As with the press cupboards, two similar Hudson Valley Kases, figure 150 and 151, make an enlightening comparison. Both are powerful, large Continental designs decorated with bold Renaissance-style rectangles, and are carried, at the front, on large bun feet. As with the two preceding examples, it is possible that both pieces were made by the same man, for many areas, such as the shaping of the grand cornices, are similar. The cupboard in figure 151 is more elaborately articulated, introducing parquetry at the center of the main door panels and re-entrant corners on the molding around them. But that in figure 150 has greater design impact. The diamond decoration on the lower part has been kept to a perfect square turned on its corner (instead of being narrowed to

a diamond form as in figure 151), creating a more forceful note, in keeping with the rectangular decoration above. Its feet, too, are more elegantly defined; narrow reel-turnings are supported by bold, exquisitely turned ball forms, whereas in figure 151 they appear bigger and less distinguished.

So far in this chapter, there would probably be general agreement on which object in each pair is the more successful. The pieces have been closely comparable, some even by the same designer. But the objects that are included as figures 152 through 157 form pairs in which each has reached the highest level of design; the choice then must be whichever of the two pleases a viewer more. The difference lies in the personalities of the object and

150

150. Kas, New York, Hudson River Valley, 1700–1735. *Courtesy of The Henry Ford Museum, Dearborn, Michigan.*

151. Kas, New York, Hudson River Valley, 1700–1735. *Courtesy of The Henry Ford Museum, Dearborn, Michigan.*

151

152

153

152. Desk, Massachusetts, Boston area, 1755–1795. *Yale University Art Gallery; The Mabel Brady Garvan Collection.*

153. Desk, Massachusetts, Boston area, 1755–1795. *Yale University Art Gallery; The Mabel Brady Garvan Collection.*

154. Side chair, Pennsylvania, Philadelphia, 1755–1795. *Yale University Art Gallery; The Mabel Brady Garvan Collection.*

155. Side chair, Pennsylvania, Philadelphia, 1755–1795. *Yale University Art Gallery; The Mabel Brady Garvan Collection.*

154

155

of the viewer, not in the quality of design.

The two Massachusetts block-front, slant-topped desks, figures 152 and 153, are equally desirable pieces; both have fine proportions, were made about the same time, and are of about equal monetary value. The designer of figure 152 has introduced a play of rounded shapes. The rounded blocking has rounded upper corners, and this is repeated in the outline of the feet and their blocking. There is an air of harmony and quiet distinction. The designer of figure 153, on the other hand, chose to establish forcefully the angularity of his object. The blocking terminates above in sharp corners that seem to emphasize the sharp corners of the case. This sharpness is introduced again by the sharply arrised knees of the dwarf cabriole legs. Each element is more immediately pronounced. Another difference can be seen in the claw-and-ball feet. In figure 152 the shaping of the reverse-curve feet seems in perfect harmony with other curved elements. In figure 153 the large feet, although considered by most collectors to be

more desirable, seem to introduce an unrelated feature, but their size is in keeping with the solidity established partly by the squareness of the parts.

Another equally excellent pair is seen in the Philadelphia Chippendale chairs, figures 154 and 155; here the difference is caused by differences in scale. Described simply, the chairs are identical: claw-and-ball feet support plain cabriole legs; a simple shell decorates the front seat rail, and a rococo shell the crest rail, which terminates in scrolled ears; the splats have identical strapwork. But although similar in description, the impact of each design is different, and each evokes a completely separate feeling. The units of the first piece are slender and elegant when compared to those of the second: the ears are smaller; the breadth of the strapwork of the back is narrower; and the knees and legs are thinner. Figure 155 is more powerful; for lack of a better description, it could be called more "masculine." A boldly bowed back terminates in great thrusting scrolled ears. These chairs

156

157

are so related in design that preference must again lie in personal taste.

The same is true of the two stands in figures 156 and 157. They are two versions, one light and one slightly heavier, of a standard Philadelphia form; but although similar they are not necessarily by the same man. Both pieces are of the highest quality, despite the fact that one has suffered minor replacements to its bird cage.

So far, we have been comparing pieces with the same basic form. The next group illustrates the designer's problems in successfully integrating construction and design. Figures 158 through 160 are not strictly related pieces, but they are card tables made at about the same time, which when compared show us much about what contributes to good design. They are all slender and elegant, yet architecturally each approaches its form in a different way.

The table in figure 158 is designed so that the vertical thrust of the foot, reeded leg, and ring-turned corner post constitute a single strong vertical element both visually and structurally; together these legs rise to support the closed double top and a shaped and decorated skirt is held between them. This construction, like that of an early house or chair, is visible and is part of the design—which contributes to making the table so successful. Figure 159, although basically of the same design, has the post part of the legs veneered to appear one unit with the skirt. That is, the light veneer carries around the corner, visually dividing the post part from the leg below; it appears as almost a separate unit. In figure 160 this division between the corner post and the leg is further established by the fact that the upper part is shaped to a rectangular unit while constructionally they are still one piece. The use of rectangular veneer panels on the corner posts further divides them from the legs, and the skirt area, including the corner posts, seems perched uneasily on the legs; the consistency of design found in figure 158 is completely missing.

Whereas the difference in success between these three card tables consisted in their allowing or not allowing the construction to be visibly incorporated into the design, in the Carver arm chairs, figures 161 to 163, it is a matter of different date and quality of manufacture. Throughout the his-

158

159

156. Stand, Pennsylvania, Philadelphia, 1755–
1795. *Yale University Art Gallery; gift of
Olive L. Dann.*

157. Stand, Pennsylvania, Philadelphia, 1755–
1795. *Yale University Art Gallery; The
Mabel Brady Garvan Collection.*

158. Card table, Massachusetts, probably Boston,
1790–1815. *Yale University Art Gallery;
The Mabel Brady Garvan Collection.*

159. Card table, Massachusetts, possibly Boston,
1790–1815. *Yale University Art Gallery;
The Mabel Brady Garvan Collection.*

160. Card table, Massachusetts, probably Salem,
1790–1815. *Yale University Art Gallery;
The Mabel Brady Garvan Collection.*

160

161

tory of furniture there is a chronological tendency toward development from heavy, forceful designs to lighter, more intricate ones. When these light, intricate designs are finally established and no further refinement seems reasonable, a major shift in styles occurs and the whole process begins again. The Carver chair in figure 161 is one of the most forceful seventeenth-century designs, although it is missing some of its original parts (the tops of the finials and the mushroom handholds). The simple front posts are decorated with ring- and reel-turnings that form a baluster shape; the front stretchers and arms terminate in ball-turnings; the rails of the back have turned line decorations, and the baluster spindles are exquisitely composed. These spindles alone are major units of design. Above and at the base they have incurvate turnings, which, at the top, cap sharp ring-turnings; the line of the baluster is bold and forceful, and the gouge-turning at mid-section is perfectly placed—had it been moved up or down a quarter

of an inch, or even an eighth of an inch, the perfect balance between the upper and lower part of the baluster would have been eliminated.

Figure 162 shows a lighter and more elegant interpretation of figure 161. The front posts have the ring- and reel-turnings, repeated on the back posts where the earlier chair had simple line turnings; the form of the handholds is an inverted interpretation of the ring- and reel-turning below, and this same unit of design is further elaborated for the finials; the top rail has been elaborated to baluster and ball forms that carry a step further the simple ring-turnings of the back rails of the earlier chair; the three balusters of the back have been made more slender and delicate, stretched out to a superb delicacy. This chair was probably made at the end of the seventeenth century and was part of the natural development from the earlier largeness of scale to the lighter designs of the William and Mary period.

The Carver chair in figure 163 is probably of

162

163

the same date as figure 162, or, with its sausage turnings, slightly later. This chair lacks any turnings of distinction: the posts are decorated with pot-like baluster forms; the handholds are not beautiful; the finials are reduced to peg-like shapes; the top rail is ill-defined; the vertical spokes of the back are of overly similar units, and there are four of them rather than the better balance of three. It might be argued that perhaps this chair came first—that finer designs were derived from it by men who saw its potential. This is not, however, the general tradition within the history of art. Such weak, attenuated shaping is characteristic of the degenerate forms that follow great forms and are the products of poor designers who misunderstand, or cannot similarly create, the genre. This last Carver chair, had it retained an interesting paint, could still have a role to play in a simple, rural restoration, for obviously not all houses contained great furniture. The piece does have something to say—but not to the art world.

CHAPTER VIII

Specialization

164

164. Daybed, Connecticut, probably Middletown area, 1755–1810. *Old Sturbridge Village photograph.*

The collecting of American furniture has been marked in recent years by a preference for pieces dating from later and later periods. From the turn of the century and up into the 1920's many collectors lived in renovated early houses, which could easily accommodate furniture of the seventeenth and early eighteenth centuries. These early collectors were interested in artifacts associated with the origins of America—the distant rather than the recent past—and they acquired pieces of furniture that easily suited their living areas and their aesthetic tastes. But as interest in the collecting of antiques became more pervasive and widespread, the scarcity of early pieces and a new understanding of later periods caused mid-eighteenth-century pieces and then later and later styles to come into fashion; recently the nineteenth century has become a major area of concentration. In part the change reflects the taste and needs of a new generation of collectors, many of whom live in larger, more elegant homes and apartments where seventeenth-century and William and Mary furniture seem out of place.

The change in taste and demand was naturally followed by a change in prices. The price of very early pieces has not risen greatly, but that of Queen Anne and later styles has soared. This trend has made later furniture seem more desirable and resulted in a misfocusing of the entire field of American furniture. The truth, of course, is that the best of each type within each period is desirable; it is simply a question of which interests the collector. In this section some specialized groups are singled out not because they have any unusual merit but because they demonstrate different ways in which a collection or area of study can be focused.

One area of design history that has not yet attracted serious students or collectors is the late expression of early forms. Many such pieces were made in the nineteenth century by cabinetmakers imitating seventeenth- and eighteenth-century ideas. The single group that has developed avid collectors is Shaker furniture.

When studying an object to discover its date of origin, it is the rule that a piece must be dated according to its latest feature, for, although an object may show many early features, its latest alone is the determining factor. Figure 164, for example, is a daybed with features that would seem to place it early in the eighteenth century; its turnings and general design apparently denote a date between 1700 and 1735. But on its crest rail there is a shell form, and the idea of placing shells on crest rails did not develop in this country until about 1740, when it became the hallmark of Queen Anne decoration. The major development of shell crest rails was in the second half of the eighteenth century, during the Chippendale period. It is therefore necessary to date the shell according to the time of its popularity. This daybed, then, must be dated after 1740, and might be as late as 1810. Another late feature is the shape of the slats of the back. Although at first these look like the slats of a bannister back, they are really narrow Queen Anne slats placed side by side.

Just as it is necessary to date an object by its latest feature, it is equally necessary to take into consideration its total attitude to design. As with the bannister back (figure 11), this daybed design is in the style of the early nineteenth century—the fancy-chair period. Although barrel forms are turned into the squared posts, everything has the sharpness and scattered quality of that later period, producing a kind of staccato effect that was part of the taste for all-over small details. It is possible, therefore, that this piece was made as

165

165. Press cupboard, northern New England, 1790–1815. *Courtesy of Israel Sack, Inc., N.Y.C.*

166. Windsor side chair, Connecticut, probably Westbrook area, 1800–1825. *Yale University Art Gallery; gift of Henry B. Stoddard.*

late as 1825 or 1830; its "atmosphere" is truly its latest feature.

Figure 165 shows a press cupboard made about 1800 that borrows its basic concept from pieces such as that in figure 27, reusing the earlier form to create a new statement. All the details point to the Early Classical Revival period, 1790–1815: the line inlay either side of the upper doors; the supporting columns of the upper section made like late clock-bonnet columns; and the square tapered legs. Further, although the doors are paneled to what seems a Renaissance idea, the bold intrusion into the panels, as in seventeenth-century work, is not present; instead, the moldings seem merely a decoration. This unusual piece with early ideas used in a late manner tells us much about seventeenth-century work, and helps us as well to understand the taste of about 1800. It is not a degeneration, or a rehash; it is a new expression that has used an earlier idea appropriately for its own time. As any piece must, it exudes the taste of its era. Intriguing as this piece is to students and collectors, however, at the time of publication it has been for sale for years, which shows how slavishly collectors allow themselves to be dictated to by current fashions in collecting. An important and fascinating collection of such pieces could still be formed fairly inexpensively by a judicious collector.

The turnings on the legs of the Windsor side chair in figure 166 seem to suggest a date between 1750 and 1800, but the medial stretcher is more elaborately turned than one might expect in the eighteenth century. A later date is firmly established by the presence of a Greek-urn form in the outer spokes of the back (this shape of classical Lecythoi became popular in America in the late eighteenth century and the early years of the nineteenth century, with the general Greek revival), and the scalloping of the lower edge and form of the top of the crest rail both suggest an early nineteenth-century fancy-chair idea. Also, like fancy chairs, the original dark paint is decorated with gold leafage on the outer back posts, the crest rail, the edge of the seat, and the baluster forms of the front legs. In addition to these specific late features, the whole impact differs from that of eighteenth-century Windsors and is consistent with early nineteenth-century taste.

166

167. Desk on frame, Connecticut, probably Hartford area, 1790–1815. *Yale University Art Gallery; gift of C. Sanford Bull.*

168. Arm chair, eastern Massachusetts or southern New Hampshire, 1750–1800. *Yale University Art Gallery; The Mabel Brady Garvan Collection.*

169. Windsor side chair, American, possibly New England, 1805–1850. *Yale University Art Gallery; The Mabel Brady Garvan Collection.*

The slant-top desk, figure 167, has an unusual design on its front. A few related pieces are known, but this is one of the strangest items of American furniture. Its date of origin is not always recognized at first. It is made with a case that rests within a stand on short cabriole legs that terminate in stylized Spanish feet; this form and construction is associated with pieces made in the first half of the eighteenth century, particularly during the Queen Anne period. The front façade seems to suggest a misconception of blocking, and blocking was popular from the late 1740's, lasting, in Connecticut, as late as 1810. It is tempting, then, to attribute the piece to a Connecticut craftsman who utilized the idea of an earlier base and, in attempting to make a blocked façade, got it backward, pushing the sides in and pulling the center out. But in looking for the latest feature it becomes evident that the recessed parts of the blocking are crowned on the top drawer by arches with scroll ends, and that these caps, with their scrolls, are like classical Ionic capitals, a feature suggesting a date of at least 1800. In further studying the façade, we realize that it does not so much misunderstand blocking as move like a serpentine front; the sides recede and the center is pushed forward. It is a personal statement of the classical taste of 1790 to 1815.

By the end of the eighteenth century many of the simpler forms, particularly chairs, had become standardized. This was partly because chairs were purchased in such great quantity that in primitive settings a standard design had become established, its rightness of design agreed upon. Such a design is figure 168, now known by the nicknames "fishtail" or "staghorn" bannister back because of the shape of the crest rail. Similar designs were made in great quantity in northeastern Massachusetts and southern New Hampshire. Their use of similar arms, turnings, and crests suggests that they were made in a simple mass-production way. But, as in any stock item made by hand, there are many minor differences. They are not all the work of one man or shop, and it is the variations that make the search for the finest examples so exciting, for when a standard form is itself a good design, the finest expression is an important discovery.

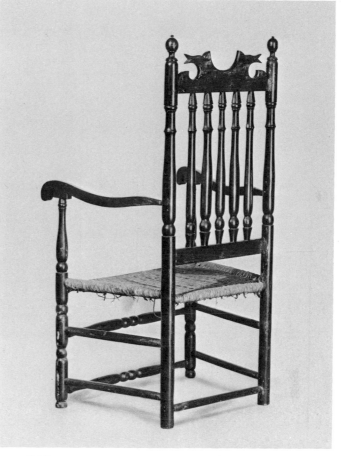

168

169

170

On the other hand, if late interpretations of early forms become a specialty, it should be remembered that not all late ideas can be justified as interesting. Just as the Carver chair, figure 163, is a bad design, so many late pieces are little more than degenerations of their exemplar. The creative collector works by recognizing the difference. The bow-back Windsor in figure 169 is a late version of such expressions as figure 142, and is great in itself because it represents not merely an imitation of its original but a rethinking of it in the idiom of its own time. In the first years of the nineteenth century, bamboo-turned stick furniture proliferated along the eastern coast of America and many examples became stock forms with little aesthetic merit. But some examples, such as this, were created by people who took this simplified form as a basis for creating objects with an incredible sense of open, simple beauty. Part of the fine design lies in the inner harmony; the legs are simply turned but their forms, with ring accents, are recalled in the turning of the medial stretcher; the simple seat holds an elegant top rail that moves nearly vertically and then breaks outward as it soars over the finely shaped spindles. The chair is not only sturdy in construction but beautiful. It is a new creation by a fine designer who has successfully transposed an earlier form to make it relevant to his own period.

The intrusion of a later time into borrowed

170. Side chair, branded "Wallace Nutting," advertised 1927. *Yale University Art Gallery.*

171. Side chair, possibly New England, 1760–1795. *Yale University Art Gallery; The Mabel Brady Garvan Collection.*

171

designs becomes a problem to those who copy furniture. The later cabinetmaker always introduced the taste of his own time, although not necessarily consciously. A maker must inevitably reflect his time, as stressed, and, unless he makes a slavish copy which would kill any spontaneity, the piece nearly always tells its own date. Figure 170 is a ladder-back chair made by the Wallace Nutting firm after Nutting had justified the existence of copies by saying that genuine Early American furniture was so scarce virtually no one could purchase it. Fortunately, some of the great collections have been formed since! But what is interesting here is not Nutting's statement but Nutting's taste, his view of the seventeenth century and of what his contemporaries thought about that period. Indeed, this chair tells us far more about Nutting's time than about the seventeenth century, for it

brings together the features that were then thought desirable in an early ladder back; the dream of the "perfect" seventeenth-century chair has created a piece that could not have existed before the twentieth century. It has massive turnings, with ball, double reel and ring finials, above multiple ring-turned back posts, connected by five arched slats, the upper one with additional shaping; in the bottom, the side stretchers are sausage-turned and the front stretcher is turned to double balusters with a central ring accent. A truly early chair with these heavy posts would be late seventeenth-century in date (and would usually be of Carver or Brewster form); it would not have had sausage-turnings, five slats, or this form of finial, all of which are early eighteenth-century forms. Even in the early years of the eighteenth century, when the ladder-back chair became more elaborately decorated, the

172

front stretchers were never turned to double balusters with a central-ring accent; this form of front stretcher appears on early bannister-back chairs and only later in the eighteenth century on ladder backs, and then usually in pairs; the use of a single stretcher of this form is again a bannister-back or Pennsylvania ladder-back conceit. Nutting combined seventeenth-century heaviness, the elaborate detailing of the early eighteenth century, and a stretcher that appeared on New England ladder backs after about 1740. When we look at it today we do not see an early concept; we see the 1920's.

Another interesting area of specialization, both from the point of view of collecting and display, is that of pieces with the same original paint color. Very effective collections of primitive furniture have been formed in this way. Some collectors, for example, picked blue paint, and since this color was particularly popular in the nineteenth century, the pieces themselves either date from then or are still earlier repainted pieces. Other collectors have specialized in decorated furniture, and others again in pieces of a particular wood. The side chair in figure 171 is obviously of tiger maple, and scattered throughout this book are other pieces made from this important American material. When finely patterned and properly used, it is one of the most exciting of wood grains available. It is a rare wood; the lumberman cannot say for sure whether a tree will have it until after felling. In this example the cabinetmaker has used the simplest of the Chippendale designs, an unbowed back, and a splat that is not pierced to strapwork. By maintaining a strict simplicity, he has allowed the wood to play the role of elaborator. Since the wavy pattern runs at right angles to the grain, it is possible to form a strong chair and have the pattern run across the shortest dimension, producing an exciting, vibrant design.

Some collectors specialize in pieces of similar wood, others in unique forms, or at least they con-

173

172. Doll's swinging double cradle, possibly New England, 1790–1815. *Yale University Art Gallery; The Mabel Brady Garvan Collection.*

173. Miniature desk, American, possibly New England, 1755–1810. *Old Sturbridge Village photograph.*

174

sider them the most exciting part of their collection. "Uniqueness" in this context generally means that a piece is the only one known of that size, or from that area; for example, the secretary in figure 52. The tiger-maple double doll's cradle, figure 172, is rare (it is the only one published to date), small, and well designed, a fine expression of the Classical Revival style of 1790–1815. The individual parts are well formed and they are combined in an interesting way. Figure 173, also a doll's object, is equally rare and fine within the primitive tradition. It is nicely scaled down, with interesting whittled wooden pulls and original blue-green paint.

A further form of collecting avidly pursued at the moment is that of labeled, stamped, branded, or signed pieces; such documented pieces, however, are not necessarily the finest. As the only known labeled John Townsend three-part dining

174.   Three-part dining table, Rhode Island, Newport, labeled "John Townsend," dated 1797. *The Rhode Island Historical Society; John Brown House.*

table, figure 174 is an extremely important document. But the greatest Newport expressions were mostly made before the Classical Revival. The form of the table is good and its inlay adequate, but it is not of the highest level; the table is now housed by The Rhode Island Historical Society, where its documentary importance is appropriately shown. One of the most interesting features of this table is the use of a center leg on the D-ends. This confirms pictorial and written evidence in establishing that early seating arrangements often placed the host and hostess at the sides rather than the ends of long tables.

In the current American furniture market, labels do astronomical things to the price of otherwise ordinary objects, and can, if the piece is a masterpiece, move it into the realm where very few can afford it. This avid seeking of documented pieces is too often carried to the extreme. The average collector would be well advised to attach much more importance to the beauty of a piece. Such considerations as where it was made and who made it, signed it, or labeled it are of secondary importance unless one is specifically purchasing for a historic setting.

CHAPTER IX

Fakes,

Reproductions,

&

Restorations

175

175. Roundabout chair, New York, New York,
1755–1795. *Yale University Art Gallery;
The Mabel Brady Garvan Collection.*

With the growing scarcity of pieces, and the continual arrival of collectors who are willing to pay prices for furniture commensurate with objects of similar rarity and beauty in other arts, the market is being flooded with material that is not what it appears to be. The creation of fakes is not something new; from the end of the nineteenth century objects that were not completely genuine were sold to collectors of Americana. One of the earliest collections, the work of the major pioneering collector Charles L. Pendleton—and which was given to the Museum of Art, Rhode Island School of Design in 1904—has in it a few objects that, although not totally wrong, have major restorations. At this distance it is impossible to know whether Pendleton himself was aware of these alterations, for it is quite likely that a piece found in an incomplete state was sold to him and restored under his direction. It is interesting that his most fraudulent pieces are English examples—probably because England had collectors of its own for over a hundred years before collecting began in America (Walpole, for example, collected elaborately turned chairs early in the eighteenth century). There was, however, from the very beginning a difference between the American and the English collector. The Englishman usually has no difficulty in judging whether a piece is English or continental; but in America there has always been the question: "Is it American or English?", or perhaps German or Portuguese, or from elsewhere. Only as collecting developed did the differences between English and American work become more evident. One of the first things to be recognized was that different woods and sometimes different constructions were used. This led to the study of interiors: it is fair to say that in many cases the early collector-scholar of American work knew more about the interior than the exterior of a piece. When he purchased something, he not only delighted in it but felt it necessary to take it apart in order to examine and understand it better. Characteristically he did not go into a shop, see a piece, like it, and take it home knowing that it was guaranteed to be genuine. He loved the challenge of fully comprehending his piece; this was part of what made collecting interesting. And in developing an understanding of the interior, he developed an awareness of what constitutes genuine wood color, and of the difference between a part stained to look old and a part which has aged over hundreds of years to a fine rich color.

On the other hand, early collectors were willing to reconstruct pieces; some were even prepared, if they found a beautiful pair of arms, to make a chair to go with them. In this sense they were far ahead of present collectors. They prized beauty to such a degree that they wanted to preserve it, to give it a context, to make it available. It is also true that some early collectors delighted in passing these reconstructed pieces off to other collectors, sometimes with genuine malice but often with the amusement that they were fooling their friends and competitors. The problem today is that many of these pieces, constructed with a love for the genuine parts, or for the delight in fooling a friend or customer, have come down to us as part of important collections that are now sanctioned by association.

With the rising prices of the late nineteenth and early twentieth centuries, fakers began their work in earnest. One of the most famous of the furniture dealers, when he arrived in this country from Europe as a penniless cabinetmaker, took a job with an antique dealer. Two of his responsibilities now cause concern. The first was to "lift" a genuine piece; that is, when the dealer found a genuine, simple piece, the cabinetmaker added elaborate inlay or carving to increase its market value. A simple Early Classical Revival card table without inlay can have its value raised many times by the addition of an eagle, or husk drops; if an expert does the work, it is difficult to know that the piece has been tampered with. Often genuine English pieces, of simple form, are altered to appear more American. This can be done by recarving the shell or feet, or by adding more American-looking inlay or interior woods. Some fakers completely reveneer a piece so that the basic form is right but the veneers are new. The result is that the interior of the piece retains its genuine early color while the exterior looks like a heavily refinished piece.

This particular cabinetmaker's second responsibility, when a person brought in a genuine piece and asked that it be refinished so that it would "look like new," was to make a copy. Since the owner wished his object to look like new, it was not difficult to return the copy to him and sell the genuine piece to someone who understood the importance and beauty of early surfaces. By this process, fakes filtered into homes in spite of the owners' firm conviction that the object had descended to them from earlier times. As these pieces now come onto the market, new problems are added. This cabinetmaker, realizing the aesthetic value of genuine American furniture, went on to become one of the dealers most concerned with authenticity.

A further problem is posed by pieces that have accumulated up to seventy years of history, genuine wear, and color change, and are associated with early collections, families, and publications; examples of this are the so-called Centennial pieces, those made during the burst of new interest aroused by the Philadelphia 1876 Centennial celebration. These pieces combined in their own way motifs from various regions and dates. A dressing table may use a Newport shell and New England blocking on a Philadelphia form with Early Classical Revival swags on a Chippendale-style case. Recently, a Centennial chest-on-chest in the Newport manner was advertised as having descended in an important Rhode Island family, as indeed it had—ever since about 1876.

The final answer is, of course, that no piece can be accepted on any grounds except its own excellence. To purchase merely because a piece has a history is as unthinking as purchasing because it "looks nice." Remember, too, that some pieces are no longer in famous collections or museums because they were found to be spurious!

Fakes fall into three general categories. First, there are the genuine pieces that have been altered so as to appear more desirable, or that were found in an incomplete state and had parts added so as to make them salable; in some cases genuine pieces are altered so that they appear to be from an area of America whose work brings higher prices. A second type of faking is done by what has been called "marrying" pieces; that is, by assembling parts that were not originally made to be together. The third type involves making a piece that is entirely new.

1. Alteration of a genuine piece.

This is the easiest and perhaps most prevalent type of faking. It can become a very sophisticated art, but at the simplest level it means taking a piece that is not particularly desirable and improving it for the market. Figure 175, a fine New York roundabout chair, was originally made as a chamber, or commode, chair. The seat rails were shaped to drop between the legs in a deep curve to conceal the chamberpot. To make this piece more desirable, the deep skirt was cut off, the lower edge filed so that it looked "properly" rough, and the newly cut surface stained to match the untouched area. In removing this deep skirt the knee brackets were also replaced. Today this fine chair, with beautifully shaped feet, may be less embarrassing to some people but it lacks the original design created by the cabinetmaker and the lower area seems too light for the upper. Figure 176 demonstrates another simple alteration that raises the price of a piece. Many people feel that late seventeenth- and early eighteenth-century chests with bun feet are more desirable than framed pieces with corner posts that simply continue behind the base molding to form the feet, or chests of board construction whose sides continue to form the feet. It has, therefore, been the custom for many, many years to saw off the extensions and put on genuine or fake bun feet. If genuine feet can be found, taken from a piece that has been largely destroyed, then it is often difficult to discern this; indeed, pieces that were made with bun feet that have since been lost are sometimes refitted with genuine feet and the substitution becomes even more difficult to spot. For other pieces, new bun feet are made and can be more easily detected. Over the years a genuine early round foot shrinks to an ovoid form; by using calipers, or sometimes simply by eye or hand, the pieces can be examined to see how far out of round they have become. But the faker tries to achieve the proper ovoid shape; new feet can be baked, creating shrinkage artificially; since the bottoms of early feet are normally checked, dark, and worn, he rubs the new feet with sandpaper, emery cloth, and stain, and then places them on a hot stove so that shrinkage, cracking, and checking are all created. The piece in figure 176 started as a simple board-construction chest over drawers; originally, the sides continued to the floor with the center cut away to form feet. Today, the bottoms of the side boards show new sawing and stain; the new bun feet are artificially ovoid in form, the bases are burned, and charcoal comes off the bottom if they are scraped.

Another variation on this type of faking is to take a genuine piece that is lacking some parts and turn it into a complete item. The piece in figure 177 began as a long looking glass with an upper and lower mirror; the upper section was a horizontal rectangle, and the lower a tall vertical. Only the top mirror remained. The faker simply took the molding that formed the bottom and moved it up to make a lower edge for the top mirror; by this simple process the piece became "all original," and no new parts are discernible.

On other pieces, carved or shaped parts are redone to make them appear to come from a different area of America. Pieces from Newport, for example, are more valuable than related pieces from Connecticut. It is therefore to the advantage of the unscrupulous to take a Connecticut piece that has shells related to Newport ones and re-create it so that it can pass as Newport.

Again, a piece can be altered so as to be more "desirable" within its own area. Until recently, Connecticut pieces were not sought by most of the major collectors. They were thought to be too complicated and busy, and often Connecticut

176

176. Chest over drawers, partly New England, 1700–1720. *Yale University Art Gallery; The Mabel Brady Garvan Collection.*

177

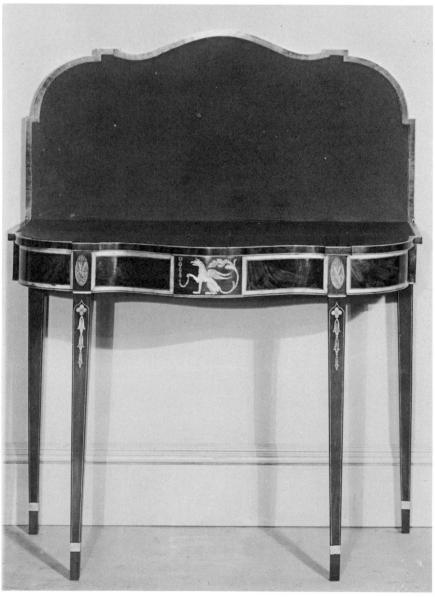

178

177. Part of looking glass, possibly English, 1690–1720. *Yale University Art Gallery; The Mabel Brady Garvan Collection.*

178. Card table, partly English, partly American, partly 1780–1800. *Yale University Art Gallery; The Mabel Brady Garvan Collection.*

pieces were "simplified" by removing some of the elaborate decoration. Now that Connecticut pieces are receiving more notice, some which started their life as a simple design are paradoxically being embellished. During a recent study of Connecticut furniture, it was found that a faker had made an amusing mistake. He had taken a piece from one area of Connecticut and in embellishing it had added decoration typical of a different area. Had he added elaboration known to have been used in the area where the piece originated it would have been far more difficult to discover the changes.

During the early part of the twentieth century, paw feet were less coveted than claw-and-ball feet. Consequently, many feet that were originally created with paws, or hairy claws, now are shaped to simple claw-and-ball feet. Today, when paw feet are recognized as rare and command considerable prestige, objects that were altered to make them more marketable early in the century would be highly prized if they had their original feet. Indeed, paw feet, sometimes early ones from English pieces, are now being added to "improve" simpler pieces.

The piece in figure 178, one of the most famous of all Baltimore tables, was recently discovered to be a genuine English table frame, mostly of oak, with new veneer and inlay. When the legs were removed they were found to have been doweled on at a later date, and the removal of the top showed it to have a different shadow mark from that which the present skirt would have created. In addition, the patterns of the inlay of the skirt and the tops of the legs were found to be early twentieth-century in taste. This table may have been the creation of a Baltimore school of fakers. They were clever enough to use enough Baltimore motifs to render the table one of the major items in the famous Baltimore show of 1947. The uniqueness of the griffin caused great excitement, but this very uniqueness should have led to a detailed study of the object as a whole.

Just as fakers have reveneered or improved existing veneer, they have also added carving. Figure 179 shows an oak chest from Texas (or possibly Germany), with later "McIntire" carving. Today, it is very clear that the scale of the basket of flowers is wrong for an early nineteenth-century design; it is too big and open in movement. The eagle on the top, however, is not unlike some nineteenth-century designs. The proof of the newness of the carving can be found by studying how it crosses the new fills between the boards of the top. The top was made of three boards that over the years had shrunk, leaving two open gaps. These gaps were filled with strips of wood and afterward the piece was carved (figure 180). The design was made with continuous lines from one board to the next, but this is what actually gave the faker away. If the carving were genuine, the lines would be continuous only when the fills were removed and the three boards pushed together. Each line should stop on one side of a fill and continue directly opposite that point on the other side.

To confirm a piece's authenticity it is always necessary to study its interior. When a piece is recarved, added to, or reconstructed, the faker usually has to refinish the exterior so that the wood colors of the old and new parts are similar. It is possible to use old wood from table tops, headboards of beds, etc., for new parts, but it is hard to match two old surfaces exactly. It is easier to sand and stain and make a uniform surface of old and new parts. Therefore, the important areas at which to look when studying a refinished piece are the interior and back: these should have no sanding or finish, and, if it is a painted piece, no paint. The interiors of cases, drawers, and seat frames, and the backs of large pieces, are of utmost importance. Here the expert searches for alterations and demands consistency of color: the inside corner of a drawer, if it is all of the same wood, should have the same color on the back, side, and bottom, where they meet. Because he knows these areas will be studied, the faker employs such tricks as varnishing the inside of a drawer or throwing ink into the corner so that it has splashed onto all the joining parts, the idea being to make it seem that the three pieces have always been together.

The need for consistent unfinished areas has given rise to one of the most interesting types of fakes, the clever and difficult practice of "saving" a highboy that has cut-down or partially destroyed legs. In many cases legs have been sawed off or shortened to make a lower piece; and in other instances fragile legs have been broken. The task

179

180

of the faker is to add new legs in such a way that all the visible wood can be refinished with the exterior, while leaving the interior untouched. To achieve this the faker must be very proficient. Generally, he proceeds as follows. Most highboys (like that in figure 12) have one continuous piece of wood running from the mid-molding to the floor, forming both the corner post of the stand and the cabriole leg. The upper parts that form the corner posts are unfinished on the inside and must not be disturbed, since any change will be immediately noticeable. It is necessary to change only the lower, cabriole part. To achieve this, the faker saws off the damaged legs just below where they join the vertical corner posts. He then tenons or dowels new legs into the bases of the corner posts and refinishes the exterior. The only area of detection is inside the stand, where the old wood of the post joins the new cabriole part; stain applied on the inner part of the saw cut helps to hide the joint.

Another favorite "improvement" is to add a bonnet or broken arch pediment to a flat-top highboy or chest-on-chest. Some genuine pieces, such as those in figures 79, 81, 83, 84, and 91, have a strong horizontal molding with a bonnet above. It is therefore possible for a faker to take a flat-topped piece and imitate a genuine form by adding a bonnet on top of the molding; this also hides the joint between the upper case and the new bonnet. Usually, however, he first removes the molding. In some instances, bonnets have been cut down to fit the piece into a low-ceilinged room, and it is then the faker's task to refashion the bonnet as he thinks it would originally have appeared. Despite the prevalence of this kind of faking, it should be remembered that sometimes a part cut off long ago still exists in an attic and can quite properly be reattached.

2. The "marrying" of sections.

The so-called marrying of sections, as the second area of faking is described, means in fact the opposite, for the two sections do not belong together. Although both are genuine, and early, each began life with a different partner. Figure 181 shows such a piece. The lower case is a fine reverse-serpentine-front slant-top desk (or the base of a secretary), made of mahogany in the

179. Chest, Texas or Germany, partly 1800–1820. *Yale University Art Gallery; The Mabel Brady Garvan Collection.*

180. Detail of figure 179.

181

second half of the eighteenth century in eastern Massachusetts. The upper case is a Pennsylvania secretary top, made of walnut, and handsomely carved with a fine shell in full relief in the center of the bonnet. When this piece was married, the faker, to increase the illusion of unity, carved into the interior door of the desk a shell similar to that in the bonnet above. The piece was then heavily refinished so that the mahogany and walnut appeared the same color. After many years the surfaces aged to their proper colors and the natural difference between mahogany and walnut became evident. Also, as time went on the carving of the lower shell became more obviously a twentieth-century creation.

In this type of faking a study of the interior colors is not sufficient, for if the top and bottom were both of similar wood they may have aged to much the same color. But different constructional methods are important: Are the drawers of the lower section made with the same form of dovetail as those of the upper sections? Are the drawer bottoms attached to the sides of the drawers in a similar way? Is similar secondary wood present in both sections? Are the tops of the sides of the drawers shaped the same way? Some cabinetmakers arched the tops, others grooved them to double arches, other finished them square or with a bead edge. Construction, and secondary woods, are usually similar in the two sections.

A further means of checking is to study the original holes for the brasses. Pieces joined together later often began with different-sized brasses, in which case the distance between the

182

181. Secretary, lower part eastern Massachusetts, upper part Pennsylvania, 1755–1795. *Yale University Art Gallery; The Mabel Brady Garvan Collection.*

182. Press cupboard, Connecticut, Durham-Madison area, 1670–1710. *Yale University Art Gallery; gift of Charles Betts.*

183

original post holes will not be the same. One of the most beautiful tiger-maple highboys known was first discovered to be married when it was noticed that the *original* post holes of the upper section were an inch farther apart than those of the lower section.

Another important area is the back. In figure 182 (the back of the press cupboard in figure 148), the upper and lower parts show a similar color, use of woods, and construction. If the sections were married, the woods might be dissimilar or the construction different; and, even if the woods were the same, the upper and lower section of two different pieces often will not have aged comparably, having undergone different climatic conditions.

A favorite faker's trick is to take the top of a William and Mary or Queen Anne highboy and add bracket feet so that it looks like an early chest of drawers. This form, although popular in England, is rarely found in America, so that when a piece such as that in figure 183 appears on the market it is immediately suspect. It could have new feet or genuine old feet from another American or English piece, or it could be completely original and a rare and desirable find. Since this form is known to be a standard faker's item, this particular chest of drawers has undergone considerable inspection, with every attempt made to prove it to be an altered highboy top. Fortunately, it has passed every test and is one of those instances where the near-unique is genuine.

3. *The totally new piece.*

The simplest way of detecting this is by the presence of circular saw marks, or, equally, of late nails or screws. But of course fakers are well aware of this. Just as the collector's passion is for the unique, the most elaborate, it is naturally the faker's, too. The making of complete fakes is apparently not as prevalent now as it was at the beginning of the collecting years, for much more is known about faking on both sides, and it is easier to make a living by improving, marrying, signing, or labeling pieces. Figure 184 shows an early fake of an almost unique form. Rarely were highboys made without drawers in the lower section, so that this piece appealed to collectors as an exciting discovery. The parts, however, are totally new, the surface being disguised by "early" red paint. "Early"-painted surfaces can be created with some degree of accuracy; fakers of country furniture specialize in crackled, worn, and "properly aged" exteriors. Sometimes the paint has glue added; when it dries, it creates "early" crackle, and undissolved powdered milk adds the "proper" texture!

People ask why, if a piece appealed to someone when he didn't know it was a fake, it ceases to be so appealing when he knows that it is not genuine. The answer seems to be that even while he appreciated it, somewhere in the back of his mind something about the object bothered him. A faker by his deliberate deception (or a copier less intentionally) adds a dimension of his own. Although this may not be evident at the time of construction, over the years the later aspect of the piece begins to stand out in relief.

Great strides are now being made in understanding fakes, partly because important collections of them are being assembled and made available to students. The collection at the Yale University Art Gallery has contributed significantly to this field of knowledge. But, in the long run, only the painstaking self-education of each collector will alleviate the problem to any great extent.

4. Foreign pieces.

A genuine piece consciously sold as something it is not may be said to represent a further form of faking: a non-American piece sold as American is quite a profitable deception.

In the discussion on the similarities and differences between English and American furniture, I have stressed that American furniture emphasized the basic line, using decoration only as an enhancement to it, whereas on developed English pieces, decoration was the pre-eminent focus, so fully de-

184

183. Chest of drawers, eastern Massachusetts, 1730–1750. *Yale University Art Gallery; The Mabel Brady Garvan Collection.*

184. Highboy, 1900–1925. *Yale University Art Gallery; The Mabel Brady Garvan Collection.*

185

186

veloped that it became itself the basic line. The danger with this statement is that country pieces were often made in England, just as in America, with little decoration, and these were also the sources of American designs. English proportions tend to be broader, boxier, and more massive; however, there are English and Continental pieces that are very similar to American products. One reason for this is that they may have come from the regions that supplied immigrants, and therefore cabinetmakers, to areas of America; for example, some parts of England provided immigrants to both Connecticut and Philadelphia, and certain likenesses between pieces in these two areas arise from their similar source of English inspiration. But, although strong similarities do exist, differences are observable, as the next three pieces show.

Figure 185 shows an English cherry ladder-back chair with features found in both Pennsylvania and Connecticut. The plain turned back posts, the arching of the slats, the form of the arms with their notched lower edge, and the shape of the front stretcher are all similar to Pennsylvania work. Typical of Connecticut are the "straight-cabriole" form of the front legs, the form of the turned foot, and the arms. The use of cherry is typical of both areas. This chair, then, could be sold as a Connecticut or Pennsylvania example by an unscrupulous dealer. In fact, it comes from the Norwich area of East Anglia and it was recently purchased in England for about one tenth of what it would have brought in America as "American." It is only by a detailed knowledge of the different turnings and shapes used in the two countries, and a feeling for what the visual experience of an American design should be, that

185. Arm chair, English, East Anglia, 1700–1750. *Yale University Art Gallery.*

186. Side chair, probably European, 1690–1740. *Yale University Art Gallery; The Mabel Brady Garvan Collection.*

187. Cupboard, Canadian, 1700–1800. *Yale University Art Gallery; The Mabel Brady Garvan Collection.*

187

we can see the difference. The chair is unlike American design in the shaping of the lower edge of the slats to double serpentines, and in this particular form of finial, although it is related to such finials as those in figure 37; also, the basic design feeling of the front posts and legs, and of the front stretcher, is English rather than American.

The side chair in figure 186, although originally purchased as American, now seems probably to have no real kinship to American products, although microanalysis suggests it might be of American wood. Unlike known American work are the deeply backward bow of the slats, the forms of the finials, the multiple ring-turnings, and the plainness of the front stretchers by comparison with such elaboration elsewhere. An exact foreign origin for this piece is not yet known, but it does relate to the elaboration found on some Scandinavian examples.

The cupboard in figure 187 was purchased as American before much was known about Canadian products, although the brass boss in the upper central panel has the raised word "Niagara" and Prince of Wales feathers. It is now known that many Canadian pieces also have this form of paneling and hinge, as well as corner posts that continue below the base molding to form feet.

Possibly no collector, museum, or dealer, even the most knowledgeable, has escaped the wiles of the faker. Such an experience is to be lived through and learned from; it is part of the process of increasing one's knowledge and sensitivity.

CHAPTER X

The Care

of

Furniture

188

Many owners of early furniture see themselves as custodians rather than mere possessors, responsible for preserving their pieces and ultimately transferring them to others who will guard them for the future. But "preservation" means many things to many people. At one extreme are those who keep pieces as they were when found; at the other are the people who want to make them look like new. How a collector or curator will act often depends upon his concept of earlier times.

It has become a traditional misconception that seventeenth-century Americans were plain, drab folks; a single glance at an unrefinished seventeenth-century piece, such as that in figure 29, will quickly dispel this notion. Reds, yellows, blacks, and indeed virtually all colors were part of the seventeenth-century way of life, and this love of color and surface enrichment continued into the nineteenth century. Thus, to remove the original color is to falsify both piece and history, and eliminate forever the knowledge of what both maker and buyer intended. Most current smooth, shiny, orange-shellacked pieces are mere shadows of their former selves.

Often a cabinetmaker had to use what woods he had at hand, or what could best be shaped to the necessary dimensions. In other cases, Windsor chairs, for example, appropriate wood was used for each different part. The legs are usually maple, since this turns to beautiful, crisp forms; the seats are usually of a soft wood such as chestnut, pine,

188. Side chair, all but restored parts possibly Connecticut, 1700–1750. *Yale University Art Gallery; gift of C. Sanford Bull.*

189. Press cupboard, partly eastern Massachusetts, partly 1670–1710. *Yale University Art Gallery; The Mabel Brady Garvan Collection.*

189

190. Highboy, eastern Massachusetts, 1715–1735. *Yale University Art Gallery; The Mabel Brady Garvan Collection.*

191. Highboy, New England, Connecticut or Massachusetts, 1715–1735. *Old Sturbridge Village photograph.*

192. Highboy, eastern Massachusetts, 1700–1720. *Yale University Art Gallery; The Mabel Brady Garvan Collection.*

190

or tulip poplar, since these woods shape easily to a saddle form; and the back is usually of hickory or ash, both of which are wiry by nature and readily bent into appropriate curves. Such variations, however, almost never showed up since the surfaces were painted and to remove the paint meant to produce something that the maker and original owner would consider unfinished.

The true custodian does not think of an early piece as something to be returned to the state in which it left the cabinetmaker, that is, smooth and newly finished; he appreciates it for what it has become. I have already criticized over-restoration. But if repairs are necessary to save the original parts and there is sufficient artistry remaining, then repairs can be justified. What is wrong is to

pass the restored piece off as completely genuine, or to add such things as bun feet to an otherwise simple piece. The ladder-back chair in figure 188, although not one of the greatest of its form, is bold, rich, and interesting, and has justifiably been restored: the legs from the floor to below the bottom ring of the front legs are new, and new lower stretchers copy those above. The legs have been continued to the floor without feet since their original form is unknown. Here a good chair has been properly saved so that the genuine parts can be appreciated, a type of restoration that should be made available to a judicious buyer at a lower price.

The opposite extreme from careful restoration is the work of the over-restorer. The press cup-

191

192

board, figure 189, was once in the Waters collection—a collection in large part ruined by the philosophy of trying to make pieces look as they did originally. Turned parts were removed, put on lathes, and sanded to crisp forms; worn parts were removed and "copied," surfaces sanded, and painted areas repainted and, surprisingly, given artificial wear. Important pieces so treated must now be considered almost as copies, for the exact forms made by the original turner and cabinetmaker are no longer known. It is, for example, impossible to tell if the quarter round nosing of the mid- and lower shelves is now exactly as the original maker intended, since it is new. The piece is not a copy, neither is it good restoration; it stands in limbo as a serious mistake by a well-intentioned collector.

To collect early pieces presumably for their particular character, and then, at great labor and expense, remove what has been purchased seems the height of absurdity. This is now a skinned cupboard with the sorry merit of recording an inadequate approach toward preserving American furniture.

Figure 190 shows a William and Mary highboy that undoubtedly was originally painted and perhaps as elaborately grained or decorated as that in figure 191. There are traces of paint, and, although the piece is of maple, the bold cove molding of the cornice, which has a drawer front, is made of pine. Early makers rarely constructed pieces of various woods unless they were to be painted (exceptions are such pieces as that in

193

figure 91), particularly when a soft wood would have been visible. Therefore, despite the crude baluster-turnings of the legs, this piece may originally have been a very exciting primitive expression. It would seem proper to repaint it to the red color of which traces exist, for this would disguise the raw yellowish maple and the pine drawer front, and reunite the surface; if properly done, the piece would reveal part of its original charm.

Figure 192, a highboy with dark Victorian varnish, is a handsome, simple piece that received little attention until it was discovered that under the late, dark varnish lay what seems to be original bold graining. It is exciting to anticipate the removal of the varnish, for what is now a bland, nicely detailed piece may become one of the most magnificent William and Mary highboys.

Figure 193 presents a different problem. It is an early eighteenth-century chest over drawers from the Hatfield area of Massachusetts, but the present paint is an early nineteenth-century redecoration (it runs over the filled brass holes on the chest section and therefore is later) and the original decoration probably exists below. The problem is, should the nineteenth-century paint be removed to expose the original surface? It is partly a matter of what exactly is underneath. If the original surface is as exciting as the top layer but no more so, then the problem still remains; and since there would be valid reason for having both, it would probably be better to do nothing. Once a paint is removed, it is gone forever.

Original, or even early, surfaces are a very important feature of early furniture, particularly on primitive and rustic pieces, as they often represent a large part of the total personality. The butterfly table in figure 194 is not one of the greatest examples of its form, its double baluster-turnings with central ring accents are not the boldest, the shaping of the "butterfly" brackets not the most exciting; but the table is united in its ap-

193. Chest over drawers, Connecticut Valley, Hatfield area, 1715–1735 (except paint). *Yale University Art Gallery; The Mabel Brady Garvan Collection.*

194. Butterfly table, New England, Connecticut or Massachusetts, 1700–1735. *Courtesy of Israel Sack, Inc., N.Y.C.*

195. Same as figure 194.

194

proach toward design, and, even more important, its surface has a marvelous patina. What is important about this table is exactly what is important about the face of a great poet or artist; it is a record of life, and may be as revealing as his work. One loves this table, instead of some other, partly because of the maker's original concept, but also because of what has happened to it. If we turn it over (figure 195), we see the marvelous consistency of color in areas that would not have been painted: the bottoms of the top, leaves, rails, and stretchers, and the insides of the rails.

The only proper care for such a piece is the application of wax (if anything must be applied). Oils, furniture polishes, and liquids of any kind are extremely dangerous as they can penetrate and permanently darken the wood. Early dealers used the famous three-part solution, which includes linseed oil, but many dealers and curators now recognize that, although at first this seems helpful, the oxidation of the oil may not only gum up the surface but turn the wood charcoal gray. There are cases of chairs from the same set that went into at least two collections, and those treated with oil are now much darker than those that were not. On certain pieces, however, oils can sometimes help.

Finally, the ability to appreciate the original visual impact is a major part of understanding Americana. A chair like that in figure 196 seems at first a shredded, tatty object, but it is important for several reasons. First, it has beautiful lines: a handsome, simple, graceful, forthright design. Second, it documents the type of gold silk damask used on such chairs and how the damask pattern was placed, for this is the original covering. Third, it is a revelation of how such chairs were sometimes studded with brass nails. It is, then, an elegant, important form, and a major example of how at least one wing chair was originally seen (the loose cushion of the seat is missing). The stripped frame (figure 197) gives us a chance to see how such pieces were made (no upholstered chair should be accepted without a study of its frame for original color, American woods, and construction). Figure 198 shows the same chair carefully restored to almost its original appearance: the original damask has been copied with considerable accuracy, and the nails replaced. This, like the restoration of the legs of figure 188,

195

shows proper attention to authenticity. It might have been tempting to use crewel work or another "early idea" on such a piece. This would not only have been inappropriate to a chair of this date and style, but would have falsified an important piece.

It is amazing how much the attention to detail can completely change an object's appearance. Figures 199 and 200 show side chairs so similar that they appear to be by one man, perhaps from the same set. The unusual feature of these Gothic-back Philadelphia Chippendale chairs is the over-upholstered seat; it was normal, on such chairs, to use slip seats which allowed a mahogany seat rail to be exposed. The wrapping of the textile over the seat rail has produced a broad, rather ungainly mass, but by using brass nails on the chair in figure 200 the feeling of expanse has been minimized and brought under control, and the front legs are tied together. Before accepting this nailing as the correct solution it would, of course, be necessary to know that there is evidence for it, in the form of original nail holes, as part of the original design; if not, it would be falsifying the cabinetmaker's concept to introduce it now.

Always we must study and try to understand the original expression, desire, and taste of the creator and his time, if we are to be fair to a piece. We decry "Sears Roebuck"-type early Americana but this, in part, is the fault of the collectors it imitates, who removed the original surface of furniture and made it "new." Too often collectors, museums, and dealers have imposed themselves on the objects instead of allowing them to remain with their own personality and raison d'être.

196

196. Upholstered arm chair, eastern Massachusetts, 1760–1795. *Courtesy of Israel Sack, Inc., N.Y.C.*

197. Same as figure 196.

198. Same as figure 196.

199. Side chair, Pennsylvania, Philadelphia, 1755–1795. *Courtesy of Israel Sack, Inc., N.Y.C.*

200. Side chair, Pennsylvania, Philadelphia, 1755–1795. *Courtesy, Henry Francis du Pont Winterthur Museum.*

197

198

199

200

CONCLUSION

One of the great museum curators, whenever he went to New York to buy American furniture, first visited the Metropolitan Museum's American Wing in order to bring his eye into focus. He deliberately attuned himself to quality so that in the shops he could more easily skip over the objects that might otherwise have excited him because of their rarity, rather than their quality of form. This tuning of the eye to the best, be it high-style, country, primitive, or rustic, must be a continual process if one is to avoid costly mistakes.

Most people go through a series of steps when looking at an object. The first is one of passionate excitement, surprise, and emotional involvement in the joy of discovery, the moment of seeing a great new piece. Because of the richness of the impact, this is a physical as well as an emotional experience, given a piece that is genuinely exciting. It then behooves the serious student or collector to "turn off" his emotions and focus his intellect. First, he should analyze the design to see what causes the initial impact. Then he should take the piece apart physically: remove all the drawers, turn the piece over, study the construction and woods, look for unexplained holes and marks, stain and new construction; try to prove, in short, that the piece is not genuine. Here the intellect must rule absolutely and no question must go unanswered.

Assuming that the piece is an exciting form and it is genuine, the third natural step is to combine the emotions and the intellect—the greatest moment of all. If the final impact seems a natural combination of these two tests, it is fairly certain that the piece will continue to excite the whole person, for it has in its design sensual perfection and absolute control so that there is no limit to the attention each feature will sustain and reward: because everything is equally perfect and perfectly balanced against everything else.

The demand for exciting forms has caused many people to buy objects which were not genuine because they did not progress to the second and third stages. It is far better to purchase part of a genuine object, when that part is itself fine, than to buy either a fake or a complete but inferior piece.

The table base in figure 201, when discovered in a small Connecticut shop, had a later top with a quarter-round molded edge, which overhung the base by just an inch or two (the base should support a cantilevered top that would overhang the ends by about a foot and a half). This incorrect restoration eliminated, to a great degree, the piece's aesthetic impact, and for some time no one paid much attention to it. Eventually a trained eye, ignoring the top, saw the splendor of the base and purchased it inexpensively. When the top was re-

201

201. Table base, Connecticut, probably New London area, 1670–1710. *Yale University Art Gallery.*

202. Leg of dressing table, New England, probably eastern Massachusetts, 1700–1735. *Privately owned.*

moved, the base sprang into being as a great form. This purchase is a good example of the selectivity possible by a trained eye that sees the bold excellence of the genuine.

Just as a part of a Greek statue—head, torso, arms, or feet—is seen as important, a fine part of a great piece of furniture is an important discovery. The William and Mary dressing-table leg in figure 202 is, first, a great form and, secondly, provides a major insight into the William and Mary period. It has perfect balance and uses the William and Mary vocabulary splendidly: the ring, reel, and baluster are beautifuly handled; the worn surface quality of the original brown paint is appealing; and its untouched condition keeps intact the chisel marks acquired when the piece was turned. The straighter areas show marks from a broad chisel; the richly shaped areas, marks from the necessarily more sharply pointed chisel. In addition, the piece has shrunk to become ovoid in cross-section as is proper on an early piece. This leg is an important document and a great sculptural form.

Finally, the simple, primitive table in figure 203 is included as an example of a deliberate change that has added to rather than distracted from the original interest of a piece. The circular top has, some time ago, been cut to one dropleaf, and a pull support installed.

Not everyone can afford the greatest objects, the finest forms; but it is possible to set one's sights on a level of good taste that one can afford to seek out. The designers of the table and the chair in figure 204 were not of the first rank. The table is nice but the legs are slightly weak in line and the chair seems overly turned without the excitement such elaboration can add. Separately, the two pieces do not reach the highest degree of quality. But placed with other similar examples, they not only reveal but exemplify a particular level of existence important in the American past. It is always possible to seek the best in an area that is currently out of fashion, as late Victorian "revival" styles are now, or in an unprestigious medium such as wicker used to be considered.

This study has attempted first to reveal the nature of American furniture and to assess its importance. Words are only a means of trying to make every piece more accessible. The critic's job

202

is to open up the beauty and significance of an object, to bring the viewer into relationship with it, not with himself. The words have no role without the object; the object always retains its own nature.

American furniture, when it is good, and a surprising amount of it is, reaches a level of personal statement that is unlike any other. The eastern seaboard of America shows us very clearly what happens when earlier forms and patterns already fully expressed elsewhere come into a vacuum where the indigenous culture is for the most part ignored. The immigrants brought with them ideas that blossomed into an entirely new statement. This came about in part because of the existence of new materials, in part because of the simplification necessary since makers tended to be less trained than their English counterparts, and in part because the life was necessarily simpler and elaborate objects therefore inappropriate. This new creation, at its best, has the utter directness of all great sculptural forms. The high-style objects are majestically self-evident; sometimes forceful and bold, sometimes serene, they are exquisitely balanced and consciously forceful in their statement, "a momentary stay against confusion." The simpler objects are either bold or delicate, harmoniously balanced, and often so warm that they become personal and intimate.

To treat such furniture simply as interesting early artifacts is one approach, but this sidesteps the pieces themselves, which should always be the original source of interest. In the last analysis, it is the object which has life and personality, and which must be confronted directly.

203

203. Table, New England, 1790–1830. *Courtesy of Roger Bacon.*
204. Roundabout chair, New England, 1710–1800; tripod stand, New England, 1750–1810. *Courtesy of Roger Bacon.*

204

Plates & Related Text

INDEX

No attempt has been made to list common furniture features (such as finials, claw-and-ball feet, or woods) except where a point is being made about them in their own right.
Numbers in italics refer to illustrations.
The following special abbreviations have been used:

Chip: Chippendale   GRR: Greco-Roman Revival   17th: Seventeenth Century   Win: Windsor
CR: Classical Revival   QA: Queen Anne   W&M: William and Mary

A Note About the Author

JOHN T. KIRK was born in West Chester, Pennsylvania, in 1933, graduated from George School in 1951, and studied cabinetmaking at The School for American Craftsmen, Rochester, New York, 1951 to 1953 and furniture design at the Royal Danish Academy of Fine Arts, Copenhagen, from 1953 to 1955. In 1955–6 he taught furniture making in a Central American work camp. He took his B.A. at Earlham College in 1959 and his M.A. in art history at Yale University in 1963. From 1964 to 1967 Mr. Kirk was Assistant Curator of The Mabel Brady Garvan and Related Collections, Yale University Art Gallery, and from 1966 to 1970 Consultant Curator for Pendelton House, Museum of Art, Rhode Island School of Design. He was Director of the Rhode Island Historical Society from 1967 through 1969 and is currently Consultant Curator of the Society's John Brown House as well as a free-lance writer, lecturer, and consultant. Mr. Kirk is the author of *Connecticut Furniture, Seventeenth and Eighteenth Centuries* (1967) and *American Chairs, Queen Anne and Chippendale* (1972).

A Note on the Type

The text of this book is set in Monticello, a Linotype revival of the original Binny & Ronaldson Roman No. 1, cut by Archibald Binny and cast in 1796 by that Philadelphia type foundry. The face was named Monticello in honor of its use in the monumental fifty-volume Papers of Thomas Jefferson, published by Princeton University Press. Monticello is a transitional type design, embodying certain features of Bulmer and Baskerville, but it is a distinguished face in its own right.